youth renewing the countryside

youth : renewing the countryside

A PROJECT OF:

Renewing the Countryside

PUBLISHED BY:

Sustainable Agriculture Research & Education (SARE)

WITH SUPPORT FROM THE CENTER FOR RURAL STRATEGIES AND THE W.K. KELLOGG FOUNDATION

SARE's mission is to advance—to the whole of American agriculture—innovations that improve profitability, stewardship and quality of life by investing in groundbreaking research and education.

www.sare.org

Renewing the Countryside builds awareness, support, and resources for farmers, artists, activists, entrepreneurs, educators, and others whose work is helping create healthy, diverse, and sustainable rural communities.

www.renewingthecountryside.org

A project of : Renewing the Countryside

Published by : Sustainable Agriculture Research and Education (SARE)

Senior Editor : Jan Joannides

Editors : Lisa Bauer, Valerie Berton, Johanna Divine

Associate Editors : Jonathan Beutler, Dave Holman, Isaac Park

Creative Direction : Brett Olson

Design Intern : Eric Drommerhausen

Lead Writers : Dave Holman and Nathalie Jordi

Lead Photographer : Dave Holman

Contributing Writers : Nancy Arcayna, Mele Anderson, Anna Barnwell, Jonathan Beutler, Laura Borgendale, Hailey Branson, Heather Foran, Kiki Hubbard, Alina Kelman, Heather Kennison, Carrie Kilman, Bryce Oates, Isaac Park, Margaret Pendleton, Amy Rathke, Elisabeth Reinkordt, Stephanie Taylor, Aubrey Videtto, Alessandra Vitrella, Erin Volheim

Contributing Photographers : Ariel Agenbroad, Maralee Bauman, Elaine Borgen, Laura Borgendale, Brad Christensen, Kiki Hubbard, Anna Jacobson, Nathalie Jordi, Jessica Marsan, Teena jo Neal, Brett Olson, Loretta Reed, Elisabeth Reinkordt, Chad A. Stevens, Jaime Winters

Advisory Team : Amalia Anderson, Jen Aspengren, Lisa Bauer, Valerie Berton, Andy Clark, Brian Depew, Johanna Divine, Jen James, Dena Leibman, Jill Martus-Ninham, Beth Munnich, Melissa Sobolik, Bouapha Toommaly, Yimeem Vu, Stephanie Weisenbach

Proofreaders and Associates : Jonathan Beutler, Sarah Brincks, Koby Jeschkeit-Hagen, Helene Murray, Isaac Park, Lindsay Rebhan, Margaret Schnieders, Kate Seager, Alison Welwood

Sponsors : Center for Rural Strategies, W.K. Kellogg Foundation

Printer : Visions Print Communications (MMSDC), Minnesota, USA

Paper : Cover, 130lb KnightKote I 30% post consumer recycled paper I FSC certified I PCF
Inside, 100lb Flo I 10% post consumer recycled paper I FSC certified

ISBN: 978-0-9795458-2-5
Library of Congress Control Number: 2009922044

Address inquiries to:
Renewing the Countryside,
612-871-1541 · info@rtcinfo.org · www.renewingthecountryside.org

Sustainable Agriculture Research and Education (SARE)
10300 Baltimore Avenue, Beltsville, MD 20705 · www.sare.org

The information given is for educational purposes only. Reference to individuals, businesses, commercial products, or trade names is made with the understanding that no discrimination is intended and no endorsement is implied by Renewing the Countryside or Sustainable Agriculture Research and Education (SARE).

First Printing

publishing partners

SARE, Youth, and Sustainable Agriculture

 A farm is to a beginning farmer what a blank canvas is to an aspiring artist. It is no wonder then that America's youth are some of agriculture's greatest innovators and experimenters. The evidence is right here between the covers of this book—youth driving rural renewal by testing new ideas on farms, ranches, and research stations across the country. SARE supports these pioneers. In this book, read about the Bauman family farm in Kansas, the Full Belly Farm in California or the Living Forestry Coop in Wisconsin, all examples of farms or projects that have received a SARE grant to test and develop new ideas—and which, in turn, have enlisted young people in their efforts. See www.sare.org/projects.

SARE is a grassroots grant making and outreach program advancing sustainable agriculture across America. SARE supports farmers, ranchers, and educators—young and old—as they explore new models for everything from clean energy farming to direct marketing to practices that protect the land and revitalize communities. SARE is grassroots: Four regional councils of top researchers, educators, and farmers set SARE policies and make grants in every corner of the nation. SARE Outreach produces and distributes practical, how-to information based on the program's more than twenty years of research results. See www.sare.org/publications.

SARE is funded by the Cooperative State Research, Education, and Extension Service (CSREES) at USDA and since its beginning in 1988 has invested a total of $161 million in more than 4000 initiatives. More than 7 percent of these grants are dedicated to fostering the next generation of farmers by helping them secure land and financing and farm more sustainably. See www.sare.org/grants.

SARE's four regional offices and outreach office work to advance sustainable innovations to the whole of American agriculture.

Renewing the Countryside

 Renewing the Countryside works to strengthen rural areas by sharing information on sustainable development, providing practical assistance and networking opportunities, and fostering connections between urban and rural citizens.

This is the ninth in a series of books Renewing the Countryside has created in partnership with others. Each book shares stories of rural renewal and all are part of an education campaign aimed at building awareness and support for the people, practices, and policies that help create healthy, sustainable, and equitable rural communities.

Other national Renewing the Countryside initiatives include:

 Green Routes— a sustainable travel program that helps diversify rural economies. The program directs people to places where they can eat, play, sleep, shop, move, and learn in ways that support a sustainable countryside. See www.greenroutes.org.

 Journeys with First Nations—like Green Routes, but on and near Indian country, in partnership with Native peoples.

In the Upper Midwest, Renewing the Countryside's work includes:

 Local Food Hero—A radio show that discusses the growing, cooking, eating, and politics of food.

 Healthy Local Foods at the EcoExperience—Educating the public about local food systems and sustainable agriculture through an innovative, interactive exhibit at the Minnesota State Fair.

 Got Local?—Networking workshops that bring together farmers and buyers of local foods.

 Creating Value-Added Communities—Facilitating communities through a process that helps them develop strategies for creating wealth and reducing poverty, while planning for sustainable economic development.

To read more stories of people revitalizing their rural communities or to learn about and support this work, visit www.renewingthecountryside.org.

table of contents

introduction

Our countryside defines America as universally as baseball, hot dogs, and apple pie and as deeply as the Statue of Liberty and the Lincoln Memorial. Whether we live in the middle of Manhattan or the suburbs of Peoria, we depend on a healthy countryside: It supplies the food we eat. It is vital to providing clean water and clean air. It is a haven for wildlife and wildflowers—a reservoir of biodiversity. It supplies the products with which we build our homes and the fibers from which our clothing is made. We flock to the countryside for recreation and rest—whether it's the slopes of the Rockies, a quiet getaway in the Northwoods, or a visit to relatives in the middle of the Heartland. Our rural areas are rich with culture, history, and hometown values that resonate with many of us.

Yet the value of the countryside has not shielded it from hard times. Rural areas and small towns have suffered from the decline in natural resource-based industries like forestry, fishing, and agriculture. The patchwork of small farms that once dominated our countryside has been replaced by large tracks of single crop farmland or paved over to make way for housing developments and shopping complexes. Communities that relied on manufacturing have seen enormous declines as jobs have moved abroad and factories have closed.

Combine lack of ready-made jobs in rural areas with young people's zest to explore the world, and it is not surprising that many of our youth head off to urban centers for education, employment, adventure, and excitement. It is not their departure that is of concern, but that most do not return. This perpetuates further decline in already aging communities. And while rural communities lament the loss of their young, they often are partly responsible. They frequently foster a climate that deters young people from joining their community. Sometimes it's a patronizing attitude towards those who return; other times it's a closed mind to new ideas or new leaders.

Young people are vital to maintaining vibrant, rural areas. We need them for their ideas, their energy, and their ability to see things differently. We need them to steward our land and our history. We need them to grow food, harvest energy, and manage our forests. We need them to help create a new, more sustainable, more just economy.

The good news is that not all smart, hardworking young people land in Seattle, Atlanta, or other urban hubs. A growing number are embracing life in rural communities and small towns. As we set out to find them, we were inspired—not only by how many we found, but by their ambition and dedication. Some are building on their history and

culture. Others are creating uniquely, twenty-first century opportunities like renewable energy businesses or Internet-based companies. Some are fighting for environmental or social justice. Many have found a foothold in building a stronger, healthier food system.

We use the word "countryside" broadly. While many of these stories come from very small towns or vast tracks of land in the West, others are set in urban areas. A piece of the countryside can prevail amidst impinging urban development; it can exist in an urban school garden or at a farmers' market.

The young people showcased here are representative of many more we didn't have room to include. The stories we have included are told by another inspiring group— young writers and photographers who beautifully captured them for these pages.

We hope this book inspires you—whether you're a teenager looking toward your future or a mom deciding what to buy for dinner. Whether you're the president of the United States or the mayor of a small town. Despite the uncertain times in which we live, these stories assure us that we can have great hope. These young people are not just renewing the countryside, they are changing the world.

— Jan Joannides, Executive Director
Renewing the Countryside

one : farming for the future

From Connecticut to California and everywhere in between, a hearty crop is taking root. And what is this groundbreaking new species? Smart, young people who are returning to the roots of American agriculture—roots steeped in a tradition and culture of diversity, quality, and respect for the earth.

While their contemporaries go off to be lawyers and doctors, teachers and computer programmers, this crop of young people sees a promising future in a new farming paradigm. Using progressive farming practices as well as time-honored traditions, they are sowing the seeds of a new agriculture, where success is measured against a triple bottom line of economic, environmental, and social considerations.

In this chapter, we meet a few of these young trailblazers who are breaking the mold, through innovation, hard work, and a commitment to living in harmony with nature. They see a future where small and mid-sized farms are a larger part of American agriculture, and rural communities draw in new people to farm.

Change is in the air. People across the country are rediscovering a passion for food grown closer to home and with a focus on quality. They want to know where their food comes from. It is this crop of clever young farmers, and those who follow in their footsteps, who are our hope—for a better food system and a healthier planet.

Before Organic

south carolina : shaheed harris

"It's like that song. You know it?" asks Shaheed Harris, who is wearing a black "Trix are for Kids" T-shirt and New Balance sneakers. "We were country before country was cool."

His soft voice peals with laughter. He's right. Shaheed's family turned back to work the land at a time when doing so was nearly unheard of, and hardly recommended. Later, they became the one of the first farms in South Carolina to become certified organic. The decision to farm was made out of necessity more than any conscious choice. Shaheed's father, Azeez Mustafa, had worked on an assembly line at DuPont and was laid off right before Shaheed was born.

"My job title was 'Group II,'" Azeez recalls. "Back in the seventies, DuPont was the highest-paying job around. Actually, it was the only job around. Either you got a job at DuPont, or you went north. Farming would no longer support a family."

After Azeez was laid off, the family lost their house, their car, and practically everything else. He built a handsawn house, in which they lived for thirteen years. They lived by lamplight, with wood fires and a kerosene stove, and became strict vegetarians—often eating raw or dumpster-salvaged food.

"Stress of mind brings expansion of mind," says Azeez, shrugging. "It was a training camp for organic farming. We grew our own vegetables and medicinal herbs, and we foraged. You know, organic, non-irrigation farming is just a poor man's way of growing food. That's how everyone used to do it, up 'til the 1960s."

According to Shaheed, South Carolina is the perfect place for growing food. Even today, Azeez's wife, Fathiyyah, claims they don't need to buy anything other than soy milk, and they use honey from a local seller instead of sugar. "There's nothing you can't grow here," he explains. "We're close to the coast and get the spin-off from hurricanes. When you see trees growing fifty-feet tall without water, you figure there must be a way for the sweet potatoes."

Irrigation, they figure, makes for plants that might grow bigger—but lack the nutrients and flavor the plants get by stretching their roots deeper into the soil to find their own water and minerals.

"Whenever we buy seeds—usually from California—the first crop is always the worst," Shaheed notes. "We save the seeds that grew successfully, and every time we replant, they adapt and become stronger. You're actually training your plant to deal with the environment. The seed is built to help itself, you know. And every generation improves."

The family uses okra seeds that originated from plants Shaheed's grandfather grew, and seeds collected from watermelons his father nurtured as a child—giving a personal meaning to the concept of "heirloom varieties."

According to Azeez, only 5 percent of the food in South Carolina is produced in the state. Emile DeFelice, a recent candidate for the position of South Carolina Commissioner of Agriculture, ran using the slogan: "Put your state on your plate!" He lost.

"And people wonder why our state is poor," Azeez veritably thunders. "If you don't support the local people, what do you think is gonna happen!"

Thankfully, local support is growing. When the family—all three generations, including Shaheed's daughter Asya—goes to the farmers' markets, they sell out every time.

"Our tomatoes don't grow perfectly round, but they taste ten thousand times better than supermarket tomatoes," says Shaheed proudly. "As long as we can get our food in people's mouths, the battle's not really with the larger farmer. But we spend a lot of time educating the consumer."

Becoming organically certified was a relatively simple matter. According to family records, the land had been free of chemicals for decades longer than the requisite three years. South Carolina State University established an outreach program

"Our tomatoes don't grow perfectly round, but they taste ten thousand times better than supermarket tomatoes. As long as we can get our food in people's mouths, the battle's not really with the larger farmer."

for minority farmers, and Clemson University helped certify the farm in 2003. A nonprofit called Carolina Farm Stewardship Association, which has been fostering sustainable agriculture since 1979, recognized the Mustafa family from the start and named them Farmers of the Year in 2006 to reward their hard work.

Today, Azeez and Fathiyyah travel and teach classes about non-irrigation farming and how to work with the weather, and other natural cycles.

After becoming certified organic, the Mustafas teamed up with eight like-minded farmers in the area to set up Sumter Cooperative Farms. To date, it is the largest organic farm cooperative in the state. The co-op continues to expand, having identified another eight farms that are on their way to being certified. They stagger the products of each grower to help them meet the demands of the market: watermelon, mizuna, and arugula are particularly sought after. Treated like living plants, the freshly picked greens stand in a pan of water, like cut flowers, until their customers pick them up.

The Mustafas specialize in salads, greens, and medicinal herbs.

"We couldn't afford to go to the doctor when Shaheed was growing up," says Azeez. "So we learned as much as possible about taking care of ourselves. We spent thirteen years without a television, remember? So we had time. Now we can afford it—but Aysa is eight and has never had to go to the doctor. You work with creation instead of against it."

What kinds of herbs keep a whole family healthy for thirty years?

"Alfalfa is the mother of all herbs—a blood cleaner," Azeez begins, counting off on his fingers: "I suggest that you use dandelion root and milk thistle to clean the liver. Cinnamon cleans the pancreas. Ginger and cayenne pepper are catalysts to clear out phlegm. Raw cranberries and thyme tea will help with kidney stones. What else? Yellow dock, burdock, echinacea, chaparral, red clover blossom. We use them all. Just use good food and herbs, and there, you've tuned the body up!"

Fathiyyah adds, "The elders still knew certain things. And the more natural you become, the more remembrances come back to you. I read Rodale, and gave it all some thought, and tested a lot of ideas. Sure, pests are a problem, but spraying gets rid of too many things. We put down grits to fight the ants; we spray with cayenne pepper, or dish detergent, or vegetable oil. The deer loved our peas and beets, but I learned that if you put human hair in your garden, they stay away." The local barbershop is happy to save up hair for Fathiyyah's natural pest management.

Minimalism and self-sufficiency are unquestioned pillars. The Mustafas have a small tractor for running rows, but family members still do most of the work by hand with a stirrup hoe.

The Mustafas farm in a way that is far more sustainable, attentive, and holistic than the industrial greenhouses in California that share the "certified organic" sticker. As organic standards loosen up increasingly, how are consumers to know the difference, when the labels look the same?

"Shop at farmers' markets," Shaheed stresses. "Buy local."

This family didn't choose organic farming for its economic or social advantages, per se. In fact, they react with what seems to be pleasant, unconcerned surprise at seeing their unusual lifestyle being adopted because, suddenly, it's hip. Whole Foods takes legions of employees on tours of the Mustafa farm, where scarecrows stand erect in the fields, glaring at animals with the effrontery to approach.

You get the feeling that, were all excitement to disappear tomorrow, the family would just shrug and carry on. But though they seem oblivious to outside forces that would shake up their world, there's nonetheless something of the prophet about both preacher-voiced Azeez and gentle Shaheed.

"Be a good shepherd," says Shaheed. "Start tearing up these beautiful yards and plant some beautiful vegetables instead! Call us if you lose the way!"

"Be a good shepherd.... Start tearing up these beautiful yards and plant some beautiful vegetables instead!"

A Piece of Rural Perfection

california : joaquina jacobo

Full Belly Farm forms a sunny patchwork of animals, plants, insects, and laborers working in collaboration to produce a bounty of crops for Sacramento and Bay Area residents. The 200-acre certified organic farm was founded in 1985 in Guinda, California, a small town about sixty miles northwest of Sacramento. The farm combines diverse agriculture with educational outreach and a firm commitment to environmental stewardship. On a typical day, Full Belly Farm hums busily as the farm's fifty or so workers tend to chicken, sheep, and cows; harvest vegetables, herbs, flowers, and nuts; and prepare boxes for CSA (Community Supported Agriculture) subscriptions beneath a hot Central Valley sun.

Joaquina Jacobo is a vital fixture on Full Belly Farm. It can be difficult to locate her with the many roles she plays, such as picking vegetables, preparing flowers for farmers markets, packing Full Belly's CSA boxes and working the farm's market stand.

"She's in the kitchen," says one worker, while another suggests she's at the washing machine. Just then, Joaquina strides from behind the shop with a wide, friendly smile and a greeting of, "Un momentito," as she rushes to drop off a wheelbarrow before moving to the cool shade to talk about her journey to Full Belly Farm.

In 1994, as a young woman, Joaquina left her parents and siblings behind in Sinaloa, Mexico, to come to the United States with her then three-year-old son, Edgar. Her husband, Bonaficio, and a job picking vegetables were waiting for her at Full Belly Farm. As a young girl, Joaquina had learned the essentials of farm work and life in the countryside while growing up on her family's small vegetable farm and cattle ranch in the mountains of Sinaloa. School was a three to four hour walk from her family home. With no car available, Joaquina was only able to attend through fourth grade. Despite her short career as a student, Joaquina sees the power of education and believes that education is the most important thing for youth to succeed.

Joaquina feels her own children, Edgar, sixteen, Briceda, thirteen, and Jose, nine, are receiving excellent educations at their school in Guinda. She'd like to see them go on to college. Fortunately, Joaquina's work on Full Belly provides an adequate living for her family and allows her children to make choices she was never afforded.

While her formal education ended early, her work on the farm and with the public has taught her valuable lessons. As a new worker, Joaquina was a shy young woman. Today, she is an "excellent communicator and facilitator," says Judith Redmond, one of the four Full Belly Farm founders. Judith describes Joaquina as focused on self-improvement—proven by her enrollment in classes to improve English skills and attain citizenship.

When she arrived at Full Belly Farm, Joaquina's primary role was picking vegetables. Today, Joaquina wears many hats, but primarily works in quality control in the farm's shop, a role she relishes. During her thirteen years with Full Belly Farm, Joaquina's abilities have evolved symbiotically with the farm's needs, capitalizing and building on her already positive and helpful nature.

"Los patrones son buenos amigos," says Joaquina as she describes her close relationship with Fully Belly Farm's owners and the family feel among the farm staff. While the work is hard, Joaquina believes she has a good job. Weekly yoga on the farm helps balance the stress involved with her work. The entire farm staff, Joaquina's sixteen-year-old son included, comes together to stretch tired muscles every Friday morning. When asked if he enjoys the yoga, Edgar says, "Yeah, it's pretty cool," a ringing endorsement from a teenager.

In contrast to Joaquina's long-term employment with Full Belly Farm, many of California's 600,000 farm workers are employed by labor contractors, and work on a temporary basis. Most are men, age twenty-five to thirty-five, who work seasonal jobs ranging from three to ten weeks. According to a National Agricultural Worker's Survey from 2003-2004, 43 percent of all individual farm workers and 30 percent of farm worker families earned less than ten thousand dollars per year.

The serenity of Joaquina's open face reflects neither the stress of hard labor nor that of parenting three children. "La vida rural es más tranquilo," she explains after considering why she chooses a rural life. Joaquina likes that she can leave keys in her car. She appreciates pure air and sees more opportunities for independence in open spaces. While she enjoys the independence of rural life, Joaquina also remains closely connected to her fellow farm workers. She makes sure that new immigrant laborers on Full Belly Farm understand the differences in United States' labor practices, such as using disinfectant liquids or working hourly instead of on contract. Joaquina's communication skills, concern for others, and deep knowledge of Fully Belly's operations make her role a natural fit.

Leaving the shady sanctuary of the garden, Joaquina walks through the farm's shop where her nearly grown son is busy sorting vegetables. She points from buckets overflowing with bright flower blossoms to the farm's fruit trees. Drying fruit lines the path while bees buzz through the grass, hard at work doing their part for the farm's production.

At the end of the orchard row are flower fields where kneeling workers are busy weeding. Finally, around the backside of the shop, Joaquina arrives at a large pile of dried garlic heads where two men sort. After a few words with them about the work they have been doing, she digs through the pile and finds what she is looking for, an enormous, brilliantly white head of garlic that is nearly the size of her small hand. Joaquina smiles, proud of the abundance she sees in a short walk around the farm. In her hand she holds a product of the farm's intensely collaborative effort, and a small piece of rural perfection.

The serenity of Joaquina's open face reflects neither the stress of hard labor nor that of parenting three children. "La vida rural es más tranquilo," she explains after considering why she chooses a rural life.

An Independent Path

minnesota : jason & laura penner

Driving to Jason and Laura Penner's farm outside of Butterfield, Minnesota, one is struck by the massive scale of agriculture carpeting the landscape. Giant wind turbines, multi-barn conventional hog operations, and endless fields of corn and soy swallow up acres upon acres. This is the modern face of Midwestern agriculture, but it is one in which human faces are strangely absent. People aren't a common feature of this landscape, unless you stop to fill up at the local gas station, or maybe visit the local school in session.

The daily reality of life on rural Minnesota's southwestern prairie is that everything seems larger than life, except for the population—especially youth. This is why the Penner family and their small-scale hog operation break the mold.

For Jason, farming wasn't always in the cards. He left his family's hog and crop farm in Minnesota to attend college in Indiana. Postcollege, he stayed in Indiana and worked as a software consultant. He also met and married Laura, a nurse from Fort Wayne. She grew up in the city, and though her grandparents had farmed, she was not accustomed to life in a rural community.

After a few years, Jason grew unhappy in his office job and decided to return to Minnesota to farm. Laura notes, "Jason told me from the beginning that he wanted to move back to the farm. I didn't know what that all entailed, but I followed."

"I really wanted to work for myself," Jason explains. "If I farmed, I would have my own business to run and could be my own manager. And I just always liked farm life."

Even with his family's support, getting into farming was a major challenge. The hurdles facing most young farmers—accessing land, getting start-up capital, finding reliable markets—can be overwhelming. So before making the leap, Jason did some very careful planning.

He researched a company he had heard about called Niman Ranch, that supplies naturally-raised pork to Chipotle Mexican restaurants, among other vendors. Niman Ranch pays farmers a premium for hogs that are raised on pasture and in deep bedding without the use of antibiotics or growth hormones. Raising hogs for Niman Ranch appealed to Jason because of the steady market and the premium paid to Niman-certified hog farmers.

As a beginning farmer, Jason was also interested in the type of hog farming that Niman Ranch promoted. The financial risks and upfront investment for raising hogs on pasture are significantly lower than raising hogs on contract in confinement barns. This made the enterprise more feasible for the Penners.

To help realize their farming dream, the Penners enrolled in the Land Stewardship Project's Farm Beginnings program, a farmer-led educational training and support program that helps people evaluate and plan their farm enterprise. Jason and Laura made the four-hour round-trip drive to attend classes every other week. The program helped them set goals, understand financial planning and marketing, and provided on-farm education from seasoned farmers. At the end of the program, they had a solid business plan and by the spring of 2004, the farm was up and running.

Today, the Penners are a bustling young family with two small sons, Ian and Aiden. Laura works part-time as a nurse in a neighboring town when she's not home with the kids. Jason has plenty of work to keep him busy on the farm, with thirty sows that he farrows twice a year and 210 acres of rented cropland planted in corn and soybeans. He also telecommutes as a software consultant for the same company he worked for in Indiana. This job provides most of his family's living, though he splits his time about half and half between the farm and his software work.

In order to achieve his long-term goal of farming full-time, Jason plans to further expand the operation. He ultimately would like to have 120 sows, which will require additional infrastructure on the farm, and, potentially, more land. Acquiring enough farmland may be one of the biggest hurdles the Penners will face, due to high prices and limited availability. Right now, Jason rents six acres from his dad that house the hoop barns and pastures, but the rest of his cropland is all rented from neighbors.

Laura explains, "The bigger farmers are just getting bigger because they have the money to buy land." This makes it difficult for beginning farmers to compete on the same playing field.

Jason is fortunate to have one landlord who charges a reasonable rent as a show of support for the young farmer and his family. But finding a support network of

"I can remember most of my kindergarten class. I think 60 or 70 percent of them all grew up on farms, and now not a single one of them is farming, except me."

young farmers has been hard for the Penners for two reasons. First, their small-scale hog enterprise stands in stark contrast to the conventional hog operations that dot their neighborhood. Second, very few young people are encouraged to enter farming. As the landscape grows more barren, with fewer neighbors, Jason can see a marked difference in the area from when he grew up.

"I can remember most of my kindergarten class. I think 60 or 70 percent of them all grew up on farms," he says, "and now not a single one of them is farming, except me."

The dearth of farmers affects not only the composition of the southwest Minnesota countryside, but also that of the rural towns that speckle the former prairie. Jason remembers going with his father to the local hog buying station, and the sense of community that was integral to the experience.

"There were just always trucks," he says. "People coming in with little livestock trailers, twenty to thirty head. There were always people talking. Now you go there, and you're basically alone."

Jason and Laura have been able to develop friendships with other young people in the surrounding communities—teachers, people in their church—but relationships with other farmers, outside of Jason's dad, have been much harder to come by. That was one aspect of the Farm Beginnings classes that Laura appreciated as they set out to farm.

"When you're surrounded with other farmers that are excited and like doing what they do, it's kind of contagious," Laura says.

"Our farm is sustainable from a standpoint of sustaining the lifestyle I want, sustaining the profitability I want, and sustaining a different way of doing things."

The Penner family is an anomaly in this age of corporate agriculture. They have taken big risks in the pursuit of their dream, but Jason knows it is worth it in the long run. "I just really chose a route that I felt could be profitable, and that would let me be independent," he says. "I don't really want to manage a ton of people. I don't want to farm by sitting in an office."

The Penner's business is well thought out. Jason comments, "Our farm is sustainable from a standpoint of sustaining the lifestyle I want, sustaining the profitability I want, and sustaining a different way of doing things."

Like any other young parent and farmer, though, Jason struggles to keep the work-life balance in check. "If the pigs are out, the pigs are out. There's no waiting 'til tomorrow. But if you can manage things right and keep your priorities straight," he adds, "it can be a really good place to have a family, and incorporate work and life together."

Survival Takes Roots

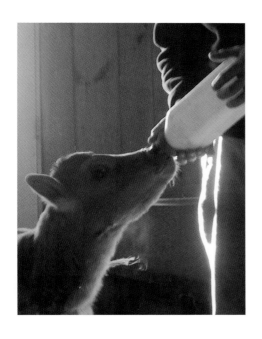

new hampshire :
chris, mike, & pat connolly

When asked how it is to work a dairy farm with his two brothers, soft-spoken Pat Connolly laughs sheepishly and answers, "A pain in the butt!"

Yet from 7 a.m. until well into the night, Chris, Mike, and Pat Connolly work as a team, constantly prioritizing and moving to the next task on the never-ending list of things to do. Jen, Chris's wife, jokes that you never see them all in the same place in a day unless there's food involved. This morning is no exception: one's baling hay, one's finishing the milking, and one's skimming cream and bottling. But at 10 a.m., they coordinate their coffee break.

It happens every morning, no matter how busy they are. Each descends from a different corner of the land to the house that they grew up in—where their parents still live, quietly keeping watch over the comings and goings down the dairy farm's dirt road. Sometimes neighbors, friends, wives, and parents join them, knowing that they'll find a few moments of warmth, caffeine, and plenty of ribbing and joking.

The Connolly brothers were twelve, ten, and seven years old when their parents ventured into farming at their home in Temple, New Hampshire, population 400 at the time. The land is shrouded in mountains, punctuated by valleys, and back then was dotted with hundreds of dairy farms throughout the county. A decade or so after they arrived, Marty and Lynda Connolly decided to launch their own dairy farm.

They had no experience, and the three boys learned alongside their parents as neighbors and friends shared insight and lent a hand. Both older brothers, Chris and Mike, left the farm to go to the University of New Hampshire but returned when it became apparent that the farm was going to need all of them in order to survive.

At one point there were five dairy farms in the town of Temple alone. Today, there are five in the entire county. Many young people can no longer afford to live on the land where they grew up, as property taxes are rising. For those who want to return to farm, the costs run high—so high that Chris remarks, "If we raise our prices any more, we won't be able to afford our own milk."

There are fewer and fewer farmers around to help new ones get started. The properties around the Connolly's that were once farmland are now estates—hilltops crowned with mansions, second homes for wealthy families. Retirees are drawn to the novelty and slower pace of New Hampshire life in comparison with the high stress of New York or Boston.

Not only that, but to be a dairy farmer, "You've got to be tough as nails," Marty states. There's mud, manure, heavy machines, and milking at all hours. The Connolly's all acknowledge that it's hard to understand what it's like until you're doing it all day, every day. But in order to hold on, this farm is no longer "just" a dairy farm. As the nearby farms go under at an incomprehensible pace, the Connolly's have converted every passion, interest, talent, logical next step, and possible idea into a business venture. They diversify to keep the farm going, and support four families in four houses.

There's the milking, of course: the 7 a.m. wake up call of uncomfortable cows. They sell their milk to HP Hood, a national distribution company that pasteurizes and distributes milk. They also sell raw milk off the farm to a loyal customer base coming from as far away as Rochester, New Hampshire, and Boston, Massachusetts. The farm store is also where they make ice cream several times a week. Lynda, Jill (Pat's wife), and Cindi (Mike's wife) come home in the evenings from working off the farm to help keep ice cream orders filled. Chris and Jen raise chickens that supply the eggs that are in high demand. Pat and Jill raise pigs and Hereford-cross cows. They sell the beef from their cattle in the store. There's a tin in the refrigerator to leave the money—all on the honor system. These are things you'd expect from a dairy farm, but there's more.

They hay the fields of their neighbors. They convert tons of manure to compost and distribute it to local gardens. On the other side of the land, Marty runs a hunting lodge and breeds pheasants, rabbits, and quail to stock the land. He and Mike have at least a dozen Bassett hounds and several rehabilitated falcons all in training. Jen runs her own carding mill, spinning yarn from the wool of neighbors' sheep. Lynda, Jen, Cindi, and Jill make pheasant pies, ice cream sandwiches, ice cream pops, sundaes, plus wool mittens, sweaters, and hats, to sell at the store.

Just when you think you would drop from the exhaustion, Pat jumps in with tales of the ski hill on their property and their work as groomers on the local mountain during the winter. Chris drives an oil truck. Mike is the fire chief. Pat is a volunteer fireman. They sit on all sorts of planning boards, determined to keep a handle on development and to advocate for their neighbors.

The farm has even won several awards, most recently as a finalist for the Green Pastures Award, which recognizes New England farms for their innovative environmental measures.

Some things remain the same for the Connolly brothers.

"Survival takes roots," Marty Connolly remarks as he surveys his sons with a mixture of awe and pride, amazed that they have chosen this life to keep the family farm surviving. The fact of the matter is that they couldn't do it without each other. They each speak with deep gratitude for their wives; for what they have sacrificed and for the radical adjustments they have made to live and work together.

The properties around the Connolly's that were once farmland are now estates—hilltops crowned with mansions, second homes for wealthy families.

To an outsider, one wonders where the hours in the day come from and how it is possible to spend so much time working as hard as they do. Yet somehow, when they're all sitting around during coffee break, they're joking with each other that none of them has a real job—and maybe they don't. They have a lifestyle—one that rolls work, play, family, love, and land all in to one.

The Noisy Little Farmer

connecticut : dan & tracy hayhurst

The name Chubby Bunny Farm conjures up a hearty laugh, but it's a serious business for master farming Connecticut couple Dan and Tracy Hayhurst. Dan, thirty-two, gets up each morning to practice something like Kung Fu, moving his arms and legs in graceful circular motions, weaving sticks or bricks into graceful patterns to get his blood flowing for the day. With this start he can attack farm work with the paradoxical combination of intense energy and patient gentleness with which all great farmers treat their land. Soft spoken and courteous, Dan smiles as he explains how Chubby Bunny got its name.

"It's sort of a joke. I guess it's a game where you put marshmallows in your mouth, and if you say chubby bunny with the most amount of marshmallows in your mouth, you win. I thought that was hilarious," he says.

The Hayhursts take a lighthearted approach to their heavy work.

Dan found it much less hilarious when he raised more than twenty rabbits for meat and they escaped into his vegetable fields. His vegetables became a veritable Mr. McGregor's garden for the many Peter Rabbits ravaging his crops. Dan and his wife, Tracy, stopped raising them because of the trouble they caused. Dan also felt uncomfortable slaughtering such an abundance of cute, small rabbits—just after tending vegetables—and decided to raise a few larger, better-behaved animals.

Now the most mischievous character at Chubby Bunny Farm is no doubt Beatrice "Butters" Hayhurst, Tracy and Dan's young daughter, whose passions include *The Noisy Little Farmer* book and ransacking their small and comfortable post and beam home. Their home abounds with fresh produce and jars of pickled or diced vegetables to last through a cold New England winter.

The Hayhursts dwell in a sheltered valley in Northwestern Connecticut, bordering on verdant wilderness preserves and removed from the hustle and bustle of the nearby metropolises. Big forested hills loom on all sides of the farm, sheltering it from the worst conditions and making for a spectacular blaze of colors each fall. Narrow country roads wind through the dense woods around the farm, occasionally opening up into the small farmsteads and homes of their few neighbors. Despite their rural location, Tracy and Dan know the big city well. About one half of their Community Supported Agriculture (CSA) clients live in New York City.

In a CSA, customers pay for "shares" in the farm and in return receive a bounty of produce on a weekly basis. The Hayhursts began delivering boxes of vegetables to the Big

"It's sort of a joke. I guess it's a game where you put marshmallows in your mouth, and if you say chubby bunny with the most amount of marshmallows in your mouth, you win. I thought that was hilarious."

Apple from land they were leasing in Stuyvesant, New York, in 2002. As this part of their business grew, Dan and Tracy became tired of the three hour drive to and from the city every week. Now that they live in a hilly rural area near their respective families where they grew up, Dan and Tracy arrange for the New Yorkers to send a truck to the farm once a week. Customers distribute the CSA goods themselves. Dan and Tracy focus more on their local community, finding nearby CSA members among former teachers, principals, and old high school friends.

When Dan needed some help on the farm one May, his older brother, Chris, volunteered. Chris writes on environmental issues and covers various adventure sports as a freelance journalist and rock climber. By the end of the summer, Chris grew to love working with his hands in the soil and cracking jokes beside his little brother. He often biked twenty-two miles each way, in addition to laboring all day on the farm.

Chubby Bunny regularly hosts farm apprentices. The apprentices appreciate Dan's eagerness not just to work hard, but also to impart his intimate knowledge of farming gleaned from internships, farm jobs, and countless hours in the fields.

The Hayhurst family grows more vegetables than they need for their CSA members, so they participate in a local farmers' market in Sheffield to sell the excess produce. They also have a little farm store in the barn where locals and CSA members come to pick up their weekly produce.

When customers arrive in the dark cool barn—built ages earlier by competent Swedish hands—they can purchase a variety of local products: homemade yogurt, organic salad dressing, pasture-raised beef. The Hayhursts love to carry other local products, as do their neighbors—marketing each other's goods at their respective farm stores. With everything from maple syrup and fresh yogurt to old-style German sauerkraut coming from nearby producers, Dan and Tracy hardly need to go grocery shopping.

Back in New York, Tracy ran the farm alongside Dan, but soon decided to follow her passion for baking. She began making cakes, pies, and cookies for the CSA members and for caterers. One year, Tracy offered dessert shares to the CSA members. Each week, members could choose between two sumptuous, hand-baked desserts. Mouthwatering as this endeavor was, it was an enormous amount of work, and the Hayhursts are back to the basics and expanding their local customer base. And now that Beatrice has a couple years under her belt, Tracy devotes less time to farming in order to pay full attention to this newest little farmer.

In diversity lies strength and stability. Dan and Tracy grow nearly sixty different types of vegetables throughout the year, ranging from staples like tomatoes and carrots to the more obscure celeriac and kohlrabi. Several dozen laying hens inhabit the same old

The Hayhursts also raise several sheep for meat, and two big, happy hogs dominate a large grass pasture. Beatrice squeals with excitement as one of the porkers squeezes himself into the muddy black water bin, grunting and snorting in this watery throne like royalty entertaining guests.

trailer that Tracy and Dan lived in for several summers on other farms. Now lined with straw, laying boxes, and proud, protective hens, the trailer is towed to a new spot every couple of days, allowing the chickens to forage on fresh grass. The Hayhursts also raise several sheep for meat, and two big, happy hogs dominate a large grass pasture. Beatrice squeals with excitement as one of the porkers squeezes himself into a muddy black water bin, grunting and snorting in this watery throne like royalty entertaining guests.

Chubby Bunny's customers appreciate Dan and Tracy's "Farmer's Pledge." They promise to adhere to strict organic standards without becoming certified organic. Dan swears off artificial pesticides, insecticides, and herbicides. Official certification demands that farmers document all of their farming decisions. For someone growing more than sixty different crops and engaging in an ingenious milieu of cover cropping, crop rotation, grazing, weeding, harvesting, and marketing, there is not a lot of time for paperwork. The Hayhursts know their customers, and their customers trust them. While organic certification can create better prices for farmers who sell crops wholesale, for now, Dan and Tracy create the same healthy organic produce for their share owners without the need for certification.

As fall approaches, the Hayhursts can look out over a good harvest and the imminent arrival of some delicious organic, free-range bacon and sausage. Dan will do odd jobs over the winter and Tracy—better with all things mathematical and official—will work on the farm's website, their taxes, and CSA membership renewals. Beatrice will continue clamoring for airplane spoonfuls of homegrown butternut squash and more readings of *The Noisy Little Farmer*.

Hay Bales & Five Generations

oklahoma : travis schnaithman

As a Dodge truck bearing Oklahoma red dirt and an "Eat Beef" license plate creeps between square hay bales, its passengers bustle with silent energy.

Behind the wheel, a youngster takes the form of a veteran farmer. His older brother scrambles across the hay towed directly behind the truck. He grins, wiping the sweat off his brow as the stack of hay on which he rides grows steadily bigger. In his eyes glows an intense pride. In his heart grows the hope of his grandfather. In his being is the making of his family's next great generation.

For this young man, twenty-year-old Travis Schnaithman, there is little question about spending the rest of his life on the farm. The Oklahoma State University agribusiness major has lived his entire life on his family's centennial farm, six miles from the rural town of Garber, Oklahoma.

The farm, Travis says, was homesteaded in 1893 by his great-great grandfather, John Jacob Schnaithman. John participated in an Oklahoma land run after immigrating to the U.S. at sixteen years of age. Five generations have been raised here since.

Abruptly turning his attention back to the hay bales, Travis lets out a laugh as younger brother, Tyler, jolts the truck to a stop announcing that it's break time.

Travis, Tyler, and three friends from Garber—persuaded by the Schnaithman brothers into helping haul hay—mosey into a tin barn and perch on hay bales. Tyler grabs a small ice chest and unveils Dr. Pepper and Gatorade. One of the friends—who graduated from Garber High School with Travis in 2005—says it's good to be back home.

"There's no place like rural Oklahoma," he says.

Another, sweating, laughs and mentions he can't remember when he last did so much physical labor. Travis takes a swig of Dr. Pepper, slaps one friend on the back, and says he loves the work.

Travis returns from college to his family's farm every chance he gets. He does pretty much everything on the farm, from driving the tractor and cleaning out wheat bins, to hauling hay and feeding cattle, to building fences. When he started at Oklahoma State in the fall of 2005, he had other ideas in mind about

how he was going to spend his life. Politics and public speaking were high on the list, but they didn't stick.

"I was so unsure about what I wanted to do, but when I came home on the weekends, there was always this excitement because I got to do what I loved and be in a place that I loved," he says.

The passion Travis has for working on the farm cannot be matched. His freshman year he made a conscious decision to return to Garber after graduating and join his family's farm. To stimulate economic development, he also plans to start an agricultural manufacturing or marketing business in Garber.

Travis says with a grin, "I realize farming is not a common career path for my generation." Many people react with surprise when they hear his plans.

He recalls a conversation he recently had with an older farmer. The man asked him about his future plans. When Travis said he wanted to farm, the man shook his head and replied, "It's a tough way to make a living."

"It's been a livelihood for generations before, and I don't want to be the generation to let it slip," Travis replied.

As he gazes across the farmland before him, Travis pauses and says slowly, "The land and the heritage mean a lot to me. It's something that just kind of gets stuck in your blood. There's been a lot of sweat and tears gone into holding onto this land."

Travis, Tyler, and their sister, Carly, were raised in the house that was built on the farm when their father, Lee, was five years old. Though Lee and his wife, Becky, live and work on the farm, Lee was the first generation to not farm full time.

Travis says his father had to pursue another career because farming had become less economically viable. While his father worked, Travis spent his childhood hiking around the farm with Myron Schnaithman, his late grandfather. Surely, it was hands-on experience that ignited his passion for the work.

"I was so unsure about what I wanted to do, but when I came home on the weekends, there was always this excitement because I got to do what I loved and be in a place that I loved."

"I was really fortunate to be around my grandpa for so long and learn from all that knowledge and wisdom and experience," he says.

From his father, though, Travis gained an enthusiasm for something else: the Future Farmers of America (FFA). Travis was playing in his parents' bedroom as a child, when one day he stumbled across a blue jacket with gold writing stitched across the chest. It was his father's high school FFA jacket. Travis decided he should get one of his own.

Joining the FFA chapter at Garber High School in eighth grade was

the beginning of a path that would hone and demonstrate his natural aptitude for agriculture. As an upperclassman, Travis served as president of the Garber FFA. His senior year, he was awarded one of organization's highest honors: 2005 State Star Farmer. He was also one of 699 FFA members to earn a State FFA Degree that year. Just before graduating, Travis was elected FFA state secretary and during the spring of 2006, he was elected state president. Though he served state-level FFA offices, Travis says his true passion lies is his own community. He has made it his personal mission to serve as an ambassador and advocate for small, rural towns.

Garber, a primarily agricultural community, boasts a population of roughly one thousand residents, many of whom—like the Schnaithmans—have been in the area for generations. Travis claims they are the finest people on earth.

"Garber's a great place to raise a family," he says. "It's a place where you don't have to worry about your kids playing in the street. I definitely want to call it home again some day."

A growing problem facing towns like Garber, though, is the fact that most young people do not come back. With the youth goes money and jobs, too.

"It's really sad," Travis says. "You go to small rural towns and all of the businesses are closed down. That's what really hurts our country. People two and three generations removed take small town heritage and agriculture for granted, and lack a sense of understanding of what small town generated products do for them."

According to Travis, the best way to revitalize small towns is to be good stewards of the land and to provide a safe and affordable environment that everybody can benefit from.

Citizens of small towns, Travis says, must also make individual efforts to support schools and to promote town image. He has tried to do his part, joining the Garber Citizens in Action. He has helped to fix old buildings, establish a citywide clean-up, and assisted with the community theater.

"A lot of people in Garber take pride in keeping Garber alive and thriving," he says. "It's a good experience to give back to the community. When I get out of college, I hope to do more of that."

As for youth returning to small towns, Travis has hope.

"History sometimes likes to repeat itself," he says. "I think that in future generations, young people will want to get out of the city so they can better understand small towns and agriculture."

The last Dr. Pepper can jangles on the bottom of an empty cooler; break time is over. The pickup is revving and Tyler motions for Travis to come. Travis smiles broadly, wipes his hands on the knees of his jeans, and gets back to work.

"People two and three generations removed take small town heritage and agriculture for granted, and lose a sense of understanding of what small town-generated products do for them."

Herbs and Heritage

texas : noemi alvarez

"I actually like weeding," says Noemi Alvarez, a week shy of fifteen. "And nobody likes weeding. But I don't like picking green beans!"

Everything coming out of her mouth sounds normal, but life is anything but for this young woman.

This will all be very confusing unless we back up a couple decades. Noemi's parents, Sylvia and Miguel, were teenagers when they came to America from Mexico in the late 1970s. Sylvia studied teaching in El Paso, and Miguel—well, Miguel was a tourist, spending a few days in Texas. He was watching some boys playing football, a sport he'd never seen, and a few minutes after joining the game, he scored a fifty-five-yard field goal. A scout signed him nearly on the spot, and he played for the Houston Oilers for a few years before starting a small dump truck business in Austin.

In 1984, Miguel and Sylvia bought ten acres of land in Lexington, fifty miles east of Austin, where the quiet landscape of neatly tilled fields is disturbed mostly by clouds of dust following pickup trucks. The soil was sandy and their land almost entirely wooded.

"You can grow watermelons here, some black-eyed peas maybe," old-timers told them. "Don't hold your breath for much beyond that."

Sylvia remembered warm milk from her grandparents' farm in Zacatecas and homegrown honey. She planted a little garden for the summer: tomatoes, peppers, squash. Surprisingly, they grew. The Alvarezes have managed to coax an amazing abundance of produce out of the sandy soil.

Noemi is the youngest of Sylvia and Miguel's three children. She was born on the farm and has helped with the family enterprise for as long as she can remember. Lucky for her, nothing about the Alvarez's farm gets boring.

Each year the view out the kitchen window changes. This is a trial-and-error family. They milked goats for a while; they raised cattle; they had a few hives of bees for mesquite honey and to pollinate the squash. They tried raising broiler chickens, then switched to quail and turkey. Last year they grew grapes, which they won't be doing again. They made strawberry ice cream and brewed tea. Harlequin bugs chomped on their arugula leaves; deer wandered in and munched on the broccoli; hawks swooped down and plucked off chickens. "It was beautiful to watch, actually," says Miguel. "But then it was like, 'Oh no, my chickens!'"

With each setback, unfazed, they reviewed their mistakes and corrected them, planting "trap crops" like early arugula to distract the harlequin bugs; building taller, electric fences to keep out the deer; and weaving an elaborate overhead spider's web of cables, beribboned with red flags, to divert the hawks.

Projects not abandoned? Herbs and heirloom tomatoes, beans, asparagus and strawberries, raised beds and French biointensive methods, and planting in sync with the biodynamic calendar developed by Rudolf Steiner. The raised beds have been the most productive. Although they lost almost three-quarters of their 800 free-range chickens to the hawks, raccoons, and foxes, they plan to persevere. This year they planted twelve thousand strawberry plants, and they'll be covering a few rows with red rather than black plastic, just to see what happens. Sylvia is the force behind such experiments.

"I read a lot," she volunteers. If Sylvia is the scientist, Noemi is her trusted lab assistant—a constant companion in the fields and co-conspirator in designing new ways to grow food more productively.

It turns out that there is little haphazard in their choices and methods.

"Chemicals destroy the land and deplete the soil," Sylvia says, "not to mention what they do to the human body."

Organic farming is more work, she adds, citing their constant battle against pests and weeds. On the other hand, by using open-pollinated heirloom seeds rather than hybrids, and foregoing chemicals, they avoid costs that conventional farmers incur.

"I'd love to farm with draft horses," she sighs, "but Miguel is the one who does all the tilling and plowing, and he likes his tractor better. You pick your battles."

"Farming is another way of worshipping God," Sylvia says, seriously. Then she chuckles: "You're close to the Creation, but you're on your knees, too!"

Noemi's perspective on farming is simpler, but no less eloquent: "I always think it's pretty awesome that from a little seed you can grow a humongous plant."

Because Sylvia has homeschooled Noemi and Miguel Jr., Noemi meets most of her friends through ballet and church. The family is of Sephardic Jewish origin. For several years they commuted to the Back to the Land ministries church in Waco, which has a number of Jewish members, but they now attend a Christian church that's closer.

"A lot of kids at church want to come to the farm because they think it's cool seeing cows, but we don't have any cows, but whatever," says Noemi, all run-on sentences, bubbly, and insouciant. "The last four rows of broccoli, my friend James from church and I planted; that was fun."

"I always think it's pretty awesome that from a little seed you can grow a humongous plant."

Miguel Jr. now attends college in Austin, but when he's at home he splits wood, kills chickens to sell, and helps with everything else. Noemi divides her time rather evenly between her schoolwork (she just finished a project on Christopher Columbus), ballet (this year she's a bon-bon in a production of The Nutcracker in Austin), and her work on the farm. Besides the ever-present weeding, Noemi helps with harvesting to get ready for two farmers' markets a week. The family has a booth at the Saturday market in downtown Austin and one on Wednesdays in front of Whole Foods, an Austin-based company.

Ninety percent of their harvest is sold at these markets; the rest goes into thirty CSA (Community Supported Agriculture) boxes.

"We'd like to do more CSAs," says Sylvia, adding that the family enjoys the personal contacts at the markets, and that new regulations will soon allow vendors to accept WIC vouchers.

Noemi chimes in, saying "The farmers' markets are cool. We know the names of all the regulars, and the kids of some of the other vendors are my friends."

The view out the kitchen window is about to change again. Enthused by the rising popularity of game birds, Miguel is planning to try raising quail again. He's hoping the income will make up for the loss of income from the large field that will be lying fallow next year—part of the plan to let fields "hibernate" every seven years. Miguel has built a clay oven to roast the quail, which he plans to sell at the farmers' market and at a new farm stand the family hopes to get up and running next summer.

"People will be able to come and pick their own strawberries," Sylvia says. Noemi nods, indicating that she'd welcome the help. Plans down the road call for building a commercial kitchen where Sylvia and Noemi can do more canning and preserving. There's also talk of constructing housing to accommodate their farm workers and perhaps WWOOFers (World Wide Opportunities On Organic Farms) or interns. Maybe they'll buy a dairy cow with their neighbors and share the unpasteurized milk. Plans are always percolating.

Meanwhile, the family is focused on a big event happening in two weeks: Noemi's quinceañera, her fifteenth birthday—a major Latin American coming of age celebration. For the past six Sundays, she and her friends have been practicing their waltz and salsa moves in preparation for the big day. The young women had long, satiny dresses made for them in Laredo; the men and boys are getting fitted for their tuxedos this weekend.

"We won't be at the farmers' market that day," says Noemi, "but we'll back the following Saturday."

Vast Promise in Montana

montana : roy & kaylee benjamin

Like the Sweet Grass Hills towering to the north of his flat farmland in North Central Montana, Roy Benjamin stands out from his surroundings. He's an astute twenty-one-year-old who started farming three years ago with his wife, Kaylee—who had been his high school sweetheart. Their land lies seventeen miles from where he grew up and this is where Roy is pioneering a new concept on old terrain.

Just outside Shelby, Montana (population three thousand), the Benjamin's home sits alone, surrounded only by miles of golden wheat stubble. Soon, all of their

2,200 acres will be certified organic—800 acres already are. Bordered by conventionally farmed land, Roy's crops are a diverse blend of dryland peas, hull-less purple barley, hard red spring wheat and hard white spring wheat.

Beyond their organic farming practices, the Benjamin's age makes them an exception in their community. The average age of farmers in rural Montana is climbing, and the fate of miles upon miles of prairie-gone-farmland is uncertain. So, too, is the economic viability of places like Shelby.

"We're kind of alone as far as people our age," Roy says with a hint of regret. "Very few neighbors' kids are interested in farming."

Roy, however, became interested early on.

"When I was in kindergarten, I wanted to be a firefighter like every other kindergartner, but by first grade, I wanted to be a farmer like no one else," he says.

Instead of college, Roy explored different farmland regions after high school, including helping with a corn harvest in Iowa. If he was going to farm, his dad told him, he should be sure about the location. His dad also told him he had to leave for two years, "to get some experience working for other people." But after just three weeks in Tacoma, Washington, where Kaylee was attending college, he was offered an opportunity to lease his neighbor's land near Shelby, and he came right home.

"Soon," Roy explains, "there will be hundreds of thousands of acres for just a handful of people interested in farming them."

What he fears is big corporations acquiring large swaths of land, and transferring business and profit from local economies to out-of-state pockets. Roy maintains hope, though, that niche markets like organic foods will help sustain small communities. He decided to certify organic primarily for economic reasons. As a new farmer in an unforgiving system, adding value to his product was a necessity.

"We have had mixed reactions to this organic deal," Roy says, "and that was one thing I promised myself when I got into it—if it doesn't work with neighbor relations, we're not going to do it. If I have weeds and they blow over the fence, I am not a good neighbor."

Roy says that the mindset of many farmers, his neighbors included, has shifted from an agronomic and ecological approach to pest, weed, and disease management to a chemical one. "As a little kid, chemicals were not a prescription," Roy says. "Now they are."

As he discusses the benefits of organic agriculture, deep-seated values become apparent. "When I'm wondering if this organic thing is really worth all the trouble, I keep reminding myself that it's my responsibility as a steward of the earth," Roy reflects. "While I need to make a living, I also need to respect what's been provided to me."

Despite jokes that he and Kaylee don't want to have kids, Roy says, "I don't want to waste it, because my grandkids might want to make a living here."

Roy has found advantages to organic farming beyond his bottom line and the health of his land. "Haul your grain to Shelby and drop it off, you never see it again. . . . It's just stuff to them. It's not food 'til it gets to Japan," he says.

"When I was in kindergarten, I wanted to be a firefighter like every other kindergartner, but by first grade, I wanted to be a farmer like no one else."

But when Roy took his first delivery of wheat to Montana Flour & Grains, a local organic buyer, they took a sample right off the truck. His wheat was baking in the oven to test the new variety before he pulled away. "So, it's food, right?" he says. "You know where it's going. That's pretty neat."

As Roy stands outside the tractor-filled barn, the notorious Northern Plains wind leaning into his back, it's obvious to the observer why he has chosen this lifestyle: it is innate to him. His commitment to this place began long before his business.

While he speaks with the wisdom of a man twice his age, Roy's youthfulness surfaces as he revs up his Freightliner semitruck with "Roy Benjamin Farm" written on the door. The roar of the engine is deafening. He beams proudly.

The question remains: how do you foster this same enthusiasm for agriculture in young people when careers in farming may not offer a paycheck each week or the assurance that bills will be paid?

"The size of this community certainly doesn't appeal to everybody," Roy admits. "But they get out there in the world, they go to college, they get a job, and they realize, 'You know, that was a really great place to be. There, people care about each other.'"

And Roy believes opportunities exist for those with an innovative spirit. "There's more room for entrepreneurship in these smaller communities than there once was," Roy says. "People willing to be

entrepreneurs have greater risks up front, but more potential for getting ahead once they have put in a few years."

Roy and Kaylee are humble about their success thus far. There are forces beyond individual control that lead to the plight of American farmers, but the decisions we make as individuals, as communities, can help preserve rural lifestyles like Roy's. Helping your community is as simple as buying from your neighbor.

"People complain about the price and availability of products in their local town as they drive fifty, sixty, a hundred miles to a Wal-Mart," Roy reflects. "They're glad to spend fifty dollars on gas to save five dollars on a pair of Nikes. If we want viable communities, we have to buy stuff in our hometowns."

But to Roy, the community experience remains all-important. People in Shelby know the person at the post office, they know the teller at the bank, and their kids are in school together.

"There's a lot of care," he says. "There's a lot of compassion. You have a genuine interest in people, and they in you."

The characteristics that define rural life are what the Benjamins hope young people will begin to see as incentives for returning to the family farm or small town.

"I would encourage other young people to take a good look at where they came from," Roy says, *"because I think a lot of them would recognize the value in the rural community and mindset."*

As Roy speaks, young and insightful, one is taken by the vastness surrounding his home. Life here is large. The plains seem to roll on without end. Squared acreage folds one on top of the other in gentle rolling sweeps, layered, interrupted only by the Sweet Grass Hills—different but welcome.

"We're very comfortable and I feel like we're as stable as we can be for this stage of life," Roy says. "Your goals change over time. There was a time that I was going to be a real conglomerate and there was another time when I wanted to live out of a garden. I guess I'm somewhere in the middle now, but we're just plain happy."

"I would encourage other young people to take a good look at where they came from, because I think a lot of them would recognize the value in the rural community and mindset."

Farm Fun & Education Fight Sprawl

maryland : candace lohr

For many local children in Churchville, Maryland, a cider smoothie from Lohr's Orchard makes a trip to the farm well worthwhile. Farm Manager Candace Lohr, twenty-eight, ensures that her family-run orchard provides more than fresh produce. Lohr's serves as a center for education and family entertainment by hosting hayrides and school trips, as well as running a lively pick-your-own business that draws people from as far away as Washington, D.C.

In the region near Baltimore, D.C., and Philadelphia, where suburban sprawl gobbles up historic farmland, Candace provides a thriving example of the economic viability of farming and the importance of agricultural leadership.

When Candace's grandfather bought land nearby their current orchard in 1928, the surrounding area was completely rural, despite its location just thirty miles northeast of Baltimore. Everyone in the family helped out with the farm work. While the landscape

has changed, the family continues to work together to grow an assortment of apples, sweet corn, peaches, tomatoes, and sweet purple plums. Candace's parents recall that before the 1950s, they grew just about every fruit or vegetable that would appear on a grocery list. Now they limit themselves. "We don't grow too many things that we ourselves don't like," says Candace.

Families from near and far flock to the orchard's wide dirt parking lot, surrounded by barns, silos, family houses, and a small pond. They come not only for the diversity of local produce, but also because of Lohr's energetic attempts to promote agritourism. Instead of just buying a bag of apples, parents can bring their kids for hayrides, to wander among the trees picking low-hanging fruit, and enjoy agricultural lessons from Candace.

Nearby kindergartens teach a fall harvest segment, and Lohr's Orchard has become an essential element of the curriculum with "Ms. Lohr" explaining basics of pollination and plant growth. Each student gets to pick two apples, and Candace also has them pick some green peaches, to help thin their peach orchard, before heading over to the mini pumpkin patch.

Not all the farm events bring laughs. Some bring screams of fear and horror. Each Halloween season the farm turns into a ghastly field of corpses, haunted by the restless souls of the Lohr family. Children alternately yelp with fright and squeal with exhilaration as they clutch their amused parents on haunted hayrides.

On less fearsome days of the summer and fall, folks walk into the Lohr's large farm store inside their big red barn and find a surprisingly diverse array of offerings. The Lohrs try to keep everything in their store local. Almost all the products come from within fifty miles of the orchard. From Keys Cheese, produced ten miles away and processed by a local Amish family, to All Natural Bone Suckin' BBQ Sauce, a diversity of locally-crafted food abounds. Jams, preserves, fresh fruit, vegetables, sauces, dressings, and more line the sturdy walls of the farm store. Screaming Hornet Sauce, Damson plum jam, garlic, and herb hot sauce, Vidalia onion dressing, pear butter, fresh peaches, cabbage, and Colby longhorn cheese draw in droves of patrons from Baltimore and D.C.

The success of the orchard comes from hard work, as well as Candace's organizational skills learned from her parents, who still work at the orchard almost every day. Candace has a bachelor's degree in accounting, but loves to work outdoors and interact with people. She works as an accountant for a couple months during the winter when things slow down at the orchard.

Candace knows her family's land creates more than just healthy food.

"I don't really think you find any better conservationists than farmers," she says. "They really are in it for the love of it. They are watching the land and taking care of it."

Despite the many hard times associated with farming, there is no end in sight at Lohr's Orchard. When asked how long Candace and her family will keep farming and direct marketing, she looks to her mother, and responds, "We'll keep going to the end."

"I don't really think you find any better conservationists than farmers. They really are in it for the love of it. They are watching the land and taking care of it."

two : flourishing entrepreneurs

Ours is a history of entrepreneurs—a country where imagination plus hard work can translate into fulfilled dreams. Small businesses are the backbone of our society. They spur local economies by creating jobs and providing needed products and services. They weave the fabric of our small towns and big cities. They create a sense of place in ways that ubiquitous corporations never can.

In this chapter, we travel to Indiana to meet a young man who started his million dollar, small town business with $400 and the Internet. We visit a couple in Missouri who opened a grocery store that specializes in local foods. We taste the success of a group of children who are learning business and life skills through running a chocolate enterprise in Utah. And we meet a lovely family of entrepreneurial, young farmers.

In Vermont, we are awed by the creativity and craftsmanship of an architect who designs and builds green homes. We meet an innovative farmer in Virginia transforming mine country into wine country. In Rhode Island, we visit an inspiring young woman building a stronger local food system.

These young entrepreneurs not only provide products and services to their communities, they are creating jobs. They are generating revenue. And their energy and vision are fundamental to the success of our small towns and rural areas. They offer hope and inspiration, and reveal the range of possibilities available to those with the dreams and tenacity to start their own enterprises.

Wheels of Change in a Rural Town

indiana : cain bond

Cain Bond named his store Peddlers Bicycle Shop, but most of his business takes place on eBay, where his professional alias terminates in "007"—a play on his last name. The business involves the intrigue, but not the espionage, of its eBay namesake.

Cain sells large quantities of strollers and bicycle parts all over the world, large enough quantities that he has grossed more than one million dollars and has had meetings with eBay's CEO. Not bad for a dyslexic twenty-year-old who started the enterprise out of his bedroom in 2004 in Washington, Indiana—a quiet rural community with a large Mennonite population. When he began the business, Cain was still in high school with just $400 in savings.

Meg Whitman, eBay's President and CEO, recently asked Cain and several other high-volume Internet vendors to attend a meeting and advise them on how to best develop the company. Cain enjoyed an all-expense-paid trip to eBay's California headquarters and the chance to share ideas with company leaders. His notoriety as the youngest participant at that meeting and other eBay vendor conferences won him nationwide media attention in magazines like *Entrepreneur*.

Cain hires employees from local schools, colleges, and the Lighthouse Mission, a local organization dedicated to helping recovering substance abusers. "They are excellent because they want a second chance and a lot of people around here won't give them a second chance," Cain says. "They're very appreciative."

Success did not come without overcoming obstacles. As a boy, Cain was challenged by dyslexia, and kids at school mocked his condition. "When I was younger, I was embarrassed about it," he says, "but by high school I got over my pride, and if I couldn't spell a word I'd ask somebody."

With his mother working side by side with him on most days in this family business, Cain ensures that the social atmosphere at the warehouse mixes serious labor and play. After he assembles a bike for sale, he takes it on a grueling and comical test ride through his warehouse, a former bowling alley, and parks it up front next to the massage tables. In addition to the bike parts and strollers, Cain assembles and sells several massage tables every week.

Many people ask Cain where he buys his merchandise and like every street-wise entrepreneur, he responds with a smile and says, "That's a secret. It's like a good fishing spot in a way. You don't want someone else showing up."

Although online sales make up around 95 percent of Cain's business, he recently decided to offer his products to local residents by opening Peddlers Bicycle Shop in the front of one of his warehouses. "It's nice to interact with people," he says. "It gives me a break from staring at the computer screen all day long."

As a grandfather and grandson walk in looking for a spare tube for the youngster's bike tire, Cain eagerly engages them in conversation. He offers local walk-in customers even lower prices than those listed on eBay.

Fundamentally, Cain's is a green business. He finds use for enormous quantities of parts and products that would otherwise go to waste or sit in storage, thus promoting the reuse and recycling of otherwise unwanted or warehoused goods. The bicycles and strollers he sells contribute to healthy lifestyles and can reduce pollution, if used as alternatives to car use. Cain believes that eBay also makes sense environmentally. When everyone would otherwise be driving all over looking for the right product, eBay allows a few FedEx trucks to do the job of hundreds of family SUVs.

Because eBay cuts out the middleman, wholesalers like Cain can sell directly to retail customers throughout the world, while providing vital income in this rural farming community. Not surprisingly, high tech Internet companies are few and far between in rural Indiana—at least for now.

Despite his success, Cain cherishes life in his home community and has no urge to do more than visit larger cities. With eBay, he has access to urban markets while still enjoying a peaceful country life with his family. Some of his buddies still tease him about how their muscular, young friend sells baby strollers, but Cain takes it all in good fun. He loves that his business allows him to transform unused excess into practical and sustainable products for people all over the nation.

Some of his buddies still tease him about how their muscular, young friend sells thousands of baby strollers, but Cain takes it all in good fun. He loves that his business allows him to transform unused excess into practical and sustainable products for people all over the nation.

A Tasty Enterprise

utah : lickety split chocolates

"This is Hubert, our VP of sales and marketing," says Lickety Split Chocolates' CEO Andrew Dayish, of a ten-year-old boy wearing a "Grim Reaper" Halloween mask.

"I am not. I'm a dead guy!" retorts Hubert Dayish, before running off for another piece of cake, a cape flapping in his wake.

All of Lickety Split's owner-operators don corporate titles and Halloween costumes, file paperwork and eat cake, equally comfortably. The fifteen children managing the tiny chocolate factory at the edges of Blanding, Utah, are a boisterous mix of the rural community's Navajo, Mormon, Mexican, and Anglo populations. The chocolate shop is set deeply within one of the nation's largest and poorest counties, the only one in Utah with a Native American majority, where 30 percent of people live below the poverty line and less than one percent of the businesses are Native-owned. But Lickety Split's children, nicknamed in one article the "White Mesa Wonkas," have sold nearly thirty thousand dollars worth of confections during their three years in business.

Tired and cheerful Elaine Borgen is the patient saint sustaining the project. Having moved to Blanding as a VISTA volunteer after twenty years in the corporate world, she remembers kids like Andrew, Creedence Sampson, Tya Manygoats, Tiffany Billie, and a few others knocking at her door to ask for money for the movies.

"I can't lend you all money," she said, "but come back tomorrow, and we'll try to figure out a way for you to make your own money."

The next day's brainstorming session led to the germination of the company's flagship product, a chocolate lollipop decorated like a traditional Navajo basket. Over the next four months, the children and Elaine made prototypes, evolved their technologies, and assigned roles: CEO, CFO, COO, president, vice president, and managers of the company's production, shipping and handling, computer, art, and sales and marketing departments.

The children meet four times a week: for after-school tutoring on Mondays and Wednesdays, and chocolate making on Fridays and Saturdays. Chocolate-making days end with a team meeting where they assess progress and discuss new schemes that have appeared on the "Chocolate Idea Board."

Older children are paid by the hour and younger ones through a point system whose monetary value changes according to the company's profits (much like stock options). Some employees earn upwards of seven hundred dollars a year. Many use the

All of Lickety Split's owner-operators don corporate titles and Halloween costumes, file paperwork and eat cake, equally comfortably.

money to help their parents with bills. Fifteen percent of the profits are reinvested for maintenance and operations. With the kids and their adult mentors registered as the Limited Liability Company's official owners, the business is listed as majority-owned Native American.

A Lickety Split spin-off has now formed on the Ute Mountain Ute reservation south of Blanding, coordinated by its director of education, Kelda Rogers. Stakeholders dream of similar franchises on reservations across the country. Increased volume could allow them to sell chocolate to such venues as the National Museum of the American Indian in Washington, D.C.

Getting out of poverty, Elaine argues, is a matter of acquiring skills and then assets. By making chocolate, the children learn from start to finish what running a business means: how to do the books, put a quality control system into place, cost a product and market it. In order to get hired, children must exceed a 2.5 grade point average, which they must also maintain if they wish to stay. But Elaine reckons the average G.P.A. for a Lickety Split employee is 3.0, and she's seen grades go up as leadership skills increase.

While the Navajo basket chocolate lollipop—which uses pure butter and cocoa butter—is still the most popular Lickety Split product, the children have also developed truffles; caramel apples presented in pretty origami boxes; hogan, teepee, and Kokopelli-shaped chocolates; chocolate-dipped strawberries and pretzels; painted pottery, and jewelry. They have opened a retail store on Main Street with funds raised by hosting a "café" with live music, desserts for sale, and pint-sized waiters and waitresses. Each year they hold a business retreat during which the Blanding and White Mesa branches of Lickety Split spend a few days together. Last year, before they traveled to the Oregon Coast, a local medicine man performed a ceremony to ensure the children's safe return.

While she's quick to laud the kids as the movers and shakers of Lickety Split, Elaine deserves much credit. She goes above and beyond, even offering breakfast at her house before school every morning to neighboring children. She works tirelessly teaching business courses at the local college, chairing the San Juan County VISTA volunteers, and pairing rural residents with business opportunities through her own VISTA project—the Legacy Community Development Corporation. Since transportation can be a challenge, many of these jobs allow people to work from home, employed by call centers or a remote-site medical coding business.

Any money made on top of her VISTA stipend (which turns out to be only 10 percent above the poverty line) is poured into Lickety Split. Once the children start turning 16, Elaine hopes to help them set up Individual Development Accounts (IDAs), bank accounts similar to a 401(k) that are matched three to one by the state. She recognizes that as a business the company is less than sustainable, leaning heavily upon her labor. The number of orders often exceeds the time the children have available to fill them, so Elaine ends up making some of the chocolates herself. But she does believe the skills that the children are learning will allow them to start sustainable businesses of their own someday.

Neither Elaine nor the kids have gone unnoticed. Generous individuals have awarded each of the kids a used bicycle and a computer, although most of them lack Internet, and some even electricity, at home. Elaine was named this year's Small Business Association's Minority Champion of the Year. The children have traveled to national conferences and been recognized by Utah senators. Creedence even met President Bush and Andrew had breakfast at the White House with Elaine.

When asked about the ways their organization differs from more traditional companies, one employee pipes up: "Our waste is about 30 percent, which is higher than at other chocolate factories, but it's hard for us to keep our hands off the chocolate!"

Indeed, a pint-sized Wonka sporting a pastry chef's floppy hat sidles up to me repeatedly with shards of white chocolate melting in her palm. Elaine maintains that Lickety Split has more to do with education than chocolate, but the children disagree: "The best thing is definitely the chocolate."

"And the people!" another pipes up.

In a no-alcohol, Mormon town where the intoxicants of choice are methamphetamines and Listerine, set in a county so big and remote it covers the same space as Rhode Island, Connecticut, and Massachusetts, with only one inhabitant for every two of its desolate, rocky square miles, a group of children get together every week to alchemize raw materials into what may look like chocolate—but is actually far more.

The phone rings, and Tya Manygoats picks up.

"Hello, Lickety Split Chocolate," she says perkily, then, annoyed, to someone in another room insolent enough to greet the same caller: "I already answered, okay?"

Then, back to the caller: "What can I help you with today?"

In a county so big and remote it covers the same space as Rhode Island, Connecticut, and Massachusetts, with only one inhabitant for every two of its desolate, rocky square miles, a group of children get together every week to alchemize raw materials into what may look like chocolate—but is actually far more.

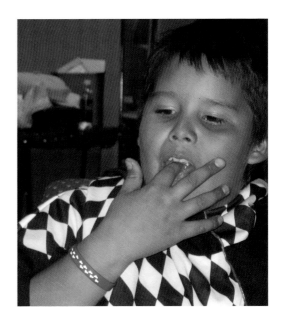

From Mines to Wines

virginia : david lawson

Rolling a tiny fruit between his fingers, David Lawson looms over a row of grapes. His tanned complexion is proof of the many hours he spends in the fields. Not so long ago, the land where David stands was barren ground—shredded by decades of coal mining. But unlike most reclaimed mine land in Wise County, Virginia, David has slowly converted the former wasteland into a prospering winery and vineyard.

MountainRose Vineyards is the product of a dream David has been developing since he was a young boy growing up in Wise, Virginia. The town of three thousand people had been home to some of the country's most lush apple orchards beginning in the 1930s, until the incursion of mining in the 1960s. Now twenty-nine, David is determined to bring back farming.

His farming career began in fourth grade, when he and a classmate sought guidance from David's grandmother. Relying on her childhood memories, they began producing molasses and apple butter. By high school, David was growing produce and even took part in creating the community farmers' market. He developed an interest in winemaking, and by the time he graduated in 1997, David had planted his first commercial acre of grape vines.

After graduation, David enrolled at Virginia Tech. Over the next few years he would attend three different universities. But David's education was in no way restricted by the university walls. At Virginia Tech, he worked at a wine cellar where he was quickly promoted to assistant winemaker. David credits this six months of hands-on experience at the winery for much of his success today. He's like a walking vintner's book, reading five separate wine periodicals each week. Along with the local library's collection of agricultural books, innumerable wine and viticulture magazines helped lay the foundation for MountainRose Vineyards.

After completing his internship, David returned to his hometown to start his winery. To prepare his land for grapes, he planted clover and tubers to replenish nutrients in the soil. Aside from the unique challenges inherent to growing on reclaimed mine land, David explains that it takes between five and eight years from the first planting until the wine is bottled and ready to be sold. During those years, he raised and sold over four thousand fall mums, annually, to generate some farm income.

By 2004, David had his first harvest. He is quick to point out that the entire project is family run. While he was the one with the vision, his parents and wife enabled his passion to reach fruition. The four worked together to build the winery and plant all the vines. His parents, Ron and

Suzanne, took an early retirement from the local school district before joining their son as winemakers. Brandi, David's wife, is doing her part too. She keeps her job as a physical therapist to pay the bills, while Mia, the couple's new baby, is sprouting into a seasoned professional grape tester.

The name MountainRose Vineyards has its own unique history that adds to David's story. The MountainRose is a seventh generation, family heirloom rose that his ancestors passed down through his family. David plants one MountainRose bush, along with a few other varieties, at the beginning of each row of wine grapes. He has discovered that the roses contract diseases before the grapes, and thus serve as an indicator that he stays keenly aware of. Beyond their history and function, the roses add glorious splashes of color that frame the endless rows of grape vines.

What sets David apart from some farmers in the area is his deep passion for the future of agriculture in Wise County. He is a proud Appalachian, with a fond respect for the mining history of the region. The theme of his winery is "Mines to Wines." David feels a responsibility "to honor some of what the mine land made possible." He knows that vineyards and wine tastings may be a new concept to his fellow Appalachians and is dedicated to reaching out to locals. With this in mind, MountainRose Vineyards wines are named after local coal seams. David tells of retired miners who come to the winery with their families and how their faces light up when they see the "Dorchester" wine—because that was the seam they had worked in.

Ten years after planting his first acre of grapes, David now has a sophisticated winery that he works constantly to improve. He grows eleven different grape varieties from which he produces nine wines. The winery is open six days a week and receives a constant flow of new visitors for the wine tastings, as well as regular customers coming to buy a couple bottles of local flavor. David also sells his wine to local restaurants, and the vineyard hosts events throughout the year, such as dinners, performances, a quilt show and cooking classes. Most recently, David's dessert wine, Autumn Gold Vidal Blanc, was awarded Best in Show at this year's Virginia State Fair.

Aside from the work he does on the vineyard, David continues to be active in the community. He currently serves as president of the local Farm Bureau and explains that his primary goal is getting farmers back to Wise County. David concedes that unlike most Farm Bureaus, his does not have enough farmers to engage in much policy work. He wants to attract enough to the area to raise policy issues. David hopes that both by example and through his work at the Farm Bureau, he will be able to inspire other young farmers to take a risk and follow their dreams.

"I was the first to put a commercial winery here," he adds. "I'm totally that person who knows what they love and what they want to do, and made a job out of doing it. You're only here once. You gotta follow your dream."

"I'm totally that person who knows what they love and what they want to do, and made a job out of doing it. You're only here once. You gotta follow your dream."

New Ideas, Old-Time Values

kansas : bauman family

Down a winding country road in Garnett, Kansas stands the Bauman farm, where agriculture is truly a family affair. Along with their parents, six Bauman children, age nine to twenty-two, take active roles in farming.

The family includes John and Yvonne, and their children, Marvin, twenty-two, Rosanna, twenty, Kevin, sixteen, Steven, fifteen, Ivin, twelve, and Joanna, nine. The Bauman's bought this farm in 2001. The farm, which is always bustling with activity, lies past the Cedar Creek Reservoir on the main road outside of Garnett. The Bauman's first farming venture as a family was to raise pastured chickens and livestock. Today, they market chickens, ducks, eggs, lamb, and beef to restaurants and grocery stores within one hundred miles of their home. The Baumans sell about 7,000 broiler chickens each year and an average of 350 dozen eggs a week.

In 2005, the family applied for a Sustainable Agriculture Research and Education (SARE) grant through the U.S. Department of Agriculture. They wanted to study the possibilities of having different species of animals pastured in the same area. Their "Multi-Species Pasture Stacking" now takes place on forty acres of pasture with permanent fencing around the perimeter. In the interior of the pasture, large paddocks are marked off by hot wire. With the "pasture stacking" project, the family increased their broiler chicken's weight by 50 percent.

Rosanna, the eldest of the girls, explains that the weight increase was due in large part to the addition of a new water system. "Beyond the benefits on the farming operation, the project had a positive social impact on us kids," explains Rosanna. "It has led each of us to take steps towards farming sustainably."

Marvin has perfected his crop rotation capabilities and established his own forty acres of certified organic cropland. Newly married, Marvin and his wife Audrey live only a few miles from the family farm. Profits from his acreage have been reinvested in equipment and machinery to sustain the farm.

Rosanna's passion is agritourism and educating others about sustainable farming. She first found interest in sharing her farm at an agritourism workshop sponsored by the state of Kansas. She then attended the North American Farmers' Direct Marketing Association's annual meeting in Texas, and came home energized to make her family's farm an agritourism destination.

The agritourism activities on the farm have grown to include a "Day on the Farm," where children come to see baby animals, help plant the year's pumpkin field, see a sheep shearing demonstration, and learn about everyday farm life. Rosanna has worked with the local chamber of commerce to market their farm in conjunction with the town's "Corn Days" celebration.

Sixteen-year-old Kevin has his own flock of sixty grass-fed sheep that he is raising on organic pastures and marketing for sale.

Pumpkins and ducks are the responsibility of the next Bauman, fifteen-year-old Steven. He is looking into the marketing opportunities for the meat and eggs from his flock of ducks. This past year, Steven also applied and received a Kansas SARE Youth Grant to study the effectiveness of using trap crops to keep squash bugs off organic pumpkins. The two acres of pumpkins that he grew were sold to grocery stores and at the fall events on the farm.

Ivin and Joanna, the youngest Baumans, are already planning their own enterprises. "I want to live in the country and farm with horses!" exclaims Ivin. As of now, he has an interest in modern production agriculture, while still utilizing historic farm

implements and heritage breeds. When Ivin isn't riding his pony, he can be found helping his older siblings with their farm projects.

"I want to raise cats," declares Joanna, the unofficial director of public relations for the farm. Joanna's youthful smile and exuberance for sharing her family's farm draws in many visitors.

The Bauman children get to know their customers, and the customers start to associate their faces with local agriculture. Belonging to the Old German Baptist Brethren, the Bauman's follow the agricultural family traditions of years' past, promoting faith, togetherness, community, and love of the land. Despite their old-time values, they take advantage of modern research and programs. They are active in the Kansas-sponsored "Simply Kansas" promotional campaign, and they work with a network of other entrepreneurial farm families.

It is through such networking that the Bauman family identified the need for more chicken processing facilities in the state of Kansas. In 2007, they opened a Kansas-certified chicken processing plant on their farm, becoming the first farmers in the state to process their own birds. Many local producers now bring their chickens to the plant for processing and the Baumans estimate they will process fifteen thousand birds per year.

The Baumans are aiming to make the plant the most sustainable chicken processing facility in the state—and perhaps the nation—by composting 100 percent of all waste and offal. Most importantly, they have slowly made progress convincing the inspectors to allow them to use less toxic chemicals. Currently, all industrially-processed chickens are bathed in Clorox before, during, and after processing. After endless cajoling, the Baumans are getting approval to use an organic-based sanitizer and another that is like hydrogen peroxide. "We are making progress little bit by little bit," says Rosanna.

The Baumans recently helped start a local farmers' market in downtown Garnett, that has exceeded their best expectations. They enjoy educating their neighbors and customers about the kind of sustainable practices they use—and just plain enjoy the hometown social interaction that the market provides.

John Bauman says about his children, "I just wanted to have a place where the kids could learn and find their own interests. Once they find their interest area, they can then build on that for their future."

The Bauman children's self-motivated work ethic is not regularly seen in today's world. Their commitment to their family, community, and customer interaction has drawn the attention of many in the local foods movement.

"Our greatest sharing times come when we give farm tours to families, retirees, and school groups," says Rosanna. "They experience a real working family farm that practices sustainable farming methods. We are always certain to educate them how we farm differently than others, and how it benefits them."

From Greenhouse to Grocery

missouri :
kimberly griffin & walker claridge

As mornings become cool and October frosts grow near, many mid-Missouri vegetable farmers race to clear their fields of the few remaining tomatoes, eggplant, okra, and green beans. The local farmers' market bustles with customers looking for that last taste of summer. Most farmers are happy to oblige, wrapping up the season and looking forward to a slower pace after months of planting, weeding, and harvesting.

But on a small, ridge-top farm overlooking Cedar Creek in rural Callaway County, Walker Claridge's harvest season is just picking up steam. In the warmth of two greenhouses, this thirty-two-year-old entrepreneur has developed an innovative food production and marketing system by focusing on the colder months. He grows a wide variety of lettuce and greens, chard, arugula, and fresh-cut herbs from October through May.

"My strategy has been to produce something when the farmers' market is gearing down for winter," he says. "People still want that good farmers' market food in November, but there's not much available."

Dubbed the "greenhouse within a greenhouse" approach, Walter's system produces his crop with almost no energy costs. He heats only a small corner of one of the greenhouses, where his germination and seeding trays spend a few weeks before being transplanted into the fertile soils of his raised beds.

"This is all about solar energy," Walter explains. "If you can collect the sun's rays and heat the ground up without allowing that warm air to escape, you're three-quarters of the way there. When it gets closer to zero, we cover our beds with another layer of plastic to protect the plants a little more."

Walter maintains that his crops can withstand freezing temperatures as long as they're not subject to the wintry winds and moisture changes outside the greenhouses. This approach provides the ultimate niche for Walter.

"Just think about Thanksgiving and Christmas," Walter suggests, "probably the two biggest food holidays we've got. What are people going to do for their Thanksgiving salad? That demand for fresh and local doesn't go away during the off-season—but the supply is almost non-existent."

"My strategy has been to produce something when the farmers' market is gearing down for winter. People still want that good farmers' market food in November, but there's not much available."

Thinking beyond his cold-weather production system, Walter and his partner, Kimberly Griffin, have developed a novel concept in marketing farm-fresh foods—owning the grocery store where local foods are sold. This approach provides them a ready market for anything and everything they can produce on their farm. In addition to their own produce, the couple stocks a full line of fruits and vegetables, meats, dairy products, eggs, jams, jellies, grains, and many other value-added products. They also sell artisan crafts and personal care products.

"We decided to go for it, and we just needed a name," explains Walter. "So we decided to call it 'The Root Cellar' to show our roots in the farming community. A generation ago, people were eating out of their root cellars for much of the year. That's where you got your potatoes and apples, your canned goods, your winter eats."

Since opening in the summer of 2001, the Root Cellar has purchased goods from more than 200 farmers. Although they prefer to purchase organic and sustainable products, The Root Cellar's "golden rule" is that, if at all possible, their products, from basil to bacon to bison burgers, come from the bounty of Missouri's varied farm and forest landscape.

"When we say local, that's what we mean," says Walter. "Sometimes we've got to stretch it slightly. I mean coffee, for instance. We've got locally-roasted coffee. That's

the best we can do on that one. How could you try to have a grocery store and not sell coffee?"

The store is able to offer a wide variety of products, everything from Missouri-grown rice to fresh trout from spring-fed Ozark creeks and ponds. They even produce their own line of gourmet salsa, marinara, and other value-added sauces.

"People come in here for the first time, and they're usually looking for some specialty goods," says Walter. "They're surprised they can pretty much get everything they need right here in Missouri. We've got almost all of your shopping list right here on our shelves."

If this all sounds like a lot of work, it is. Walter and Kimberly spend countless hours managing both the farm and the grocery store.

"We've tried it all," says Walter. "I mean, we had the breakfast and lunch café thing going for a while. We've done deli foods and sandwiches. We've done a lot of catering jobs."

Now, with their son, Lushen, nearing the age of two, the couple is revamping The Root Cellar with a streamlined approach to achieving their goals. They recently completed a move from a larger location with kitchen facilities to a smaller storefront in a high-traffic area. The new location is in the heart of downtown Columbia, a vibrant community of specialty shops, restaurants, and other retail establishments. In addition to reaching more shoppers, the new Root Cellar site has cut expenses due to reduced rent and utility rates.

"We're in good shape in the new location," Kimberly explains. "Our customer base is well-established. We have some good people trained to run the store. Now we can focus on doing more of the farming. That's always been our plan. Get the Root Cellar up and going and on solid ground; then start producing more of the food sold in the store on our own farm."

Reflecting on the way their dual approach to production and marketing has developed, Walter notes the organic nature of the process.

"It's not like we went into this thing with all of the answers," he says. "We saw some things happening. First, you've got a huge demand for local products that is not being met by conventional grocery stores. Second, you've got the ability to produce good food pretty much year round. We finally just took the risk and jumped in head-first."

For many farmers dependent upon commodity markets, vertical integration is a dirty concept signaling low prices paid to farmers and increased profits for corporate agribusiness. For Walter and Kimberly, owning the produce system from the seed to the grocery store shelf has meant capturing every bit of the consumer dollar. That is their recipe for success, and if you ask them, it's the best tasting recipe you're likely to find—even if it wasn't exactly the way you planned it.

Has it been easy? "No way!" says Walter. "But we've made a decent living and we're doing what we love. We get to be our own boss. I don't know how you can put a dollar value on that, but it's worth every penny."

Has it been easy? "No way!" says Walter. "But we've made a decent living and we're doing what we love. We get to be our own boss. I don't know how you can put a dollar value on that, but it's worth every penny."

Simple Materials, Grand Designs

vermont : ben graham

The trees Ben Graham uses to build timber frame homes never lose their character; in fact, they don't always lose their limbs either. Instead, branches become braces, knots become artwork, and natural shapes interlock to form solid joints. Ben started Natural Design Build in 2001, with a focus on ecological building techniques. He has become well-known in the region for pushing forward innovative designs. Ben's work balances aesthetically appealing design with the use of low impact materials and techniques, while keeping costs affordable. His meticulously hand-drawn blueprints slowly transform imagination into creation and offer insight into Ben's steadily growing business in Plainfield, Vermont.

Ben grew up in a cooperative house with his mother and father in Cleveland. He wishes Plainfield had the ethnic and cultural diversity he experienced in Cleveland, but that doesn't stop him from being active in his Vermont community. As a boy, he loved drawing Japanese animation cartoons, castles, and samurai he found in encyclopedias. When he opened an architecture book in his school library, he was fascinated by the structures and forms that flowed from its pages. "There was a phase when I was just going to the library and finding cool photos I liked," he says.

This "phase" became the passion that spawned his eventual career. From his ramblings in books and interest in drawing, an idea of what he wanted to do with his life slowly percolated. When he had the opportunity to attend college, Ben enrolled in the Rhode Island School of Design as an architecture student. Armed with his five-year architecture degree and certification from the Permaculture Institute of Britain, Ben set off to turn blueprints into structures and dreams into reality. Like plans for any custom-built structure, his blueprints and schematics take on a life of their own, evolving with his buildings as they rise from their foundations.

Ben drafts architectural plans in his unique studio home—the old Plainfield fire station. An old firefighter's helmet hangs at the top of his stairs near a large, Japanese-style wooden bar, carved out of a single, gorgeous piece of wood. The spacious, loft-like structure embodies much of Ben's personal philosophy. A custom built woodstove and masonry chimney heat the entire space. Subtle artistic touches make the firehouse feel alive, graceful, and even spunky in its old age.

The first floor houses his workspace and drafting area, lined with tools of the trade and scroll-like blueprints from past creations. The second floor serves as a kitchen and living room and has a ladder leading up to a cozy loft. A new timber-framed bedroom addition brings a Japanese aesthetic together with Viking and Hobbit influences, using local eastern white cedar. Ben added this addition, not just as an experiment, but because he needed a proper bedroom for his fiancé. Ascending the ladder above the loft, a peaceful view of Plainfield unfolds from the cupola: old New England houses cluster the main streets, small shops abound, while a lazy river flows through the center of the bucolic village. Outside, Ben built a wood-fired hot tub that overlooks the river.

Before Ben came to Plainfield, he spent some footloose years working as a builder on projects throughout the country, mostly in the West. One of his favorite projects is what he dubbed the Castle Pine Half Moon Shrine, a stunning Japanese shrine set in a reflective garden. Ben and his helpers crafted the graceful structure from simple wood, clay, stone, glass, and earth. Its sharply edged roof angles sweep towards the sky, while colorful light from a small stained glass window dapples the dome's white interior. The shrine uses only natural materials and symbolizes harmony between the physical and spiritual worlds. Like many of Ben's creations, the shrine directly reflects the landscape and garden designed around it.

Ben's interest in Japanese style and form fully blooms in another house project in New Hampshire. From the building's spacious, light-filled interior, visitors look out over 125 acres of New Hampshire forest. It features not one, but two round wooden roofs that sweep effortlessly over sturdy beams and smooth adobe-like straw bale walls. The central pillar in the house is not a squared post, but a whole debarked tree with three branches reaching out to brace the structure. It twists like a living tree supporting leafy limbs and a staircase spirals around it. The lowest level of the three-story house is anchored in the ground by large stones that slope up from the earth to the beginning of the smooth walls. The walls support the distinctive conical wooden roofs and hand-carved rafters. Ben likens them to the gills on the underside of a mushroom as they radiate out from the center of the roof.

"There's just something balanced and pleasing to the eye," he explains.

One of the team helping to build the New Hampshire house is Brooke Ray, a young woman carpenter from Burlington. Ben differs notably from the many builders who rarely employ women. He tries to involve women in building projects because they bring a different energy to a job site, and they work just as hard and skillfully as men. New Frameworks Natural Builders, a company of two female straw bale experts, is another frequent partner.

In addition to the New Hampshire house, Ben simultaneously adds the finishing touches to a timber-frame home in Berlin, Vermont. In this project, the eyes are immediately drawn to gaze at the enormous tree trunk craned into place as the ridge beam. The mighty trunk measures more than twenty-four inches in diameter. It's wide enough for Ben to nimbly scamper along it like a soaring catwalk. He carries a large chain saw thirty-five feet above the ground for the final adjustments to the supporting rafters. When asked about the death-defying act, Ben smiles, and explains that he and his fellow timber framers take great pride in their tradition of aerial building. Like the giant ridge timber in Berlin, almost all of the timbers and wood Ben uses on his projects come from the site. At the New Hampshire house, the site was logged in winter by a local forester and a team of draft horses. Ben explains that this building is healthier to live in than a conventionally-built home, and contrary to widespread misinformation about green homes, costs roughly the same and will last many times longer.

This building is healthier to live in than a conventionally-built home, and contrary to widespread misinformation about green homes, costs roughly the same and will last many times longer.

Imagine a half-million dollar dream home built without a single sheet of plywood, pressure-treated lumber, or toxic glues. Instead it consists of natural, rot-resistant materials harvested from within a couple miles of the site. Despite success building larger eco-dream homes, Ben grows frustrated with houses of several thousand square feet for just one or two people. His desire for the future is to accept only projects that appeal to his sense of appropriate scale.

Soon, the first level of Ben's firehouse will transform into the Spiralworks gallery, a venue for all types of artists to explore and display works bridging culture and nature. Spiralworks began as a nonprofit venture Ben shared with some friends. They've since taught several natural building workshops and contemplated buying a lilac farm to serve as a community center. Ben now hopes the gallery will help establish his hometown of Plainfield as a center for sustainable living design; one that draws tourists, students, and artists from around the region. With Ben's service on the planning commission, his work on new building innovations, and his recruitment and training of young crafters, Plainfield may become more than just a center of the arts. Perhaps it will also be a hub for aspiring and creative young builders who can make homes that are healthier for people, for the land, and will last hundreds of years.

As Farm Fresh Rhode Island grew, it made its priority outreach to urban communities that have a hard time finding affordable fresh foods. The organization partners with local churches, YWCAs, and community centers to put up informational flyers. They sponsor talks about the markets, and how local produce can be affordable, yet healthy and delicious. Although Rhode Island is a small state, this is no small task for Farm Fresh Rhode Island. Louella knows that although a generation of new farmers' markets now operate without their help, many more have yet to be organized.

Farm Fresh Rhode Island also organizes conferences throughout the year for farmers, restaurant buyers, and food activists to shares ideas and brainstorm new ways to reinvigorate the market for local food. Louella says, "We want to fertilize the ground for a new generation of farmers, and our belief is that young people will turn towards farming if it's a viable occupation."

Just when Farm Fresh Rhode Island was rolling forward at a steady pace, the call of the land and the long days at the office began to get to Louella. She had noticed that Rhode Island had no locally-made cheese in the entire state. After an internship at the Appleton Creamery, a goat cheese operation in Maine, Louella returned to Providence in 2007, to cofound Narragansett Creamery. She can now be found at the cheese vats stirring her curds and whey, and watching Farm Fresh Rhode Island continue to blossom.

When asked what she'll do next she simply says, "Anything that's connected to food and farmers' markets. I could do this for the rest of my life."

three : embracing heritage

Preserving culture, carrying on traditions, these are things often relegated to older generations. At some point, most young people drift away from, or outrightly reject, the beliefs and customs of their families and communities. This is true whether you live in a small town, or in a large city. It is part of growing up: to cast off the familiar and seek your own truths.

Seeking these truths sometimes brings people full circle to see the value and wisdom within their own culture. Other times, it introduces them to different traditions and cultures with which they resonate.

This chapter explores the lives of young people who are whole-heartedly embracing culture and heritage. For some, like the Quileute fisherman in Washington, it is relearning the traditions of his ancestors—traditions that have been around for hundreds of generations. For others, like the young cattlewoman in Nevada, it is recognizing that the traditions with which she was raised are on the decline, and working to share these and the unique history and heritage of the American West with others.

These stories bring hope. They show how young people can respect and recognize the wisdom of their elders and ancestors, while incorporating current day realities and knowledge. They demonstrate that young people are capable of an incredible depth of spirit, intelligence, and commitment.

Reviving Tradition

washington : dakwa woodruff

Dakwa (pronounced "Day-kwa") Woodruff is a role model in the seaside Quileute tribe of Washington's Olympic Peninsula. At the age of twenty-seven, he proudly owns two of his own fishing boats and even more proudly named the first vessel after his daughter, Shilaily. While some fishermen on the West Coast are in their fourth or fifth generation, Dakwa could be the four hundredth generation, as archeological evidence and Quileute fishing culture dating back thousands of years attest.

"Our ancestors were fishermen, oceangoing people. We're just trying to pick up the first steps of our ancestors," he says.

The forty-eight-foot Shilaily is a wooden vessel outfitted for long lining, trawling, and crabbing. Built in Tacoma during the 1950s, it undergoes fastidious maintenance and yearly hull sandings by Dakwa's father, among others.

"The old sea dogs around here recognize it even though she's got a new name," Dakwa remarks proudly. "They tell me: 'You got a really good seaworthy boat here.'"

What looks like a calm day in the harbor at La Push may create dangerous seas even for boats as large as Dakwa's. The Shilaily uses long lines for halibut, salmon, and black cod that stretch for up to three miles. Trolling far up and down the coast of Washington, they often bring back ten to twenty thousand pounds of seafood for each day on the water. Dakwa and his crew also deploy over six hundred crab traps into which crawl the large and delicious Dungeness crabs that make the area famous. After several good years and hard work on the Shilaily, Dakwa bought another boat, the fifty-six-foot Seactis, also Dakwa's Quileute name.

For several years, Dakwa studied natural resource management at Bellingham College, but decided to return to the reservation and begin working as a deckhand on fishing boats. In 2003, he purchased the Shilaily and refitted her for fishing. Few families work as closely as Dakwa's. The two boats are crewed by his sister Sharra, and his cousins Fred, Jason, Scott, Ryan, and Dylan. Dakwa's father now captains the Shilaily, as Dakwa steers the Seactis.

After stocking up with plenty of bait and several tons of ice, they will be on the water by 7 a.m. and return around 4 p.m. Many fishing trips extend for two, three, and even four days, flooding the Shilaily's hold with seawater and crustaceans that are sold still alive. With the new boat, they're hoping to land up to thirty thousand pounds on two-day outings.

When Dakwa first acquired the Shilaily, his family decided that it needed to be "wiped off" with Quileute blessings and ceremonies. His mother, Jill, is very knowledgeable about natural medicine, herbal remedies, and Quileute ceremonies. She led the family in a blessing ceremony for the boat by burning sage, a plant sacred to scores of Native American tribes, and offering prayers to the newly named Shilaily.

Once, after a string of mechanical failures and minor accidents, Dakwa decided it was time to renew the blessing and underwent another ceremony for the boat. Afterwards, the crew felt better in their hearts and there were no more mishaps onboard.

"I knew in my mind, something got done by that blessing," Dakwa says.

In addition to leading healing ceremonies and important rituals, Jill cooks traditional foods on a scale many chefs never approach. She often cooks for dozens or hundreds of tribal members at potlatches (community feasts), and once even cooked traditional food for the U.S. Congress.

As a member of the Quileute tribe, Dakwa operates under the Treaty of Olympia signed January 6th of 1856. The treaty guarantees fishing rights to tribal members for all time. This allows Dakwa to avoid the same crab trap and other restrictions placed on non-Native fishermen.

"A lot of guys don't like us because they think we've got it made, but they don't realize that that was our way of life." Dakwa explains.

Unless Native American fishermen exercise their treaty rights, they stand to lose them altogether. Although Dakwa never hears overt racism on the radio channels at sea, he wryly admits that strong racial tensions often surface in the fishing community on the Washington coast. Dakwa, though, doesn't let such things get in his way.

Dakwa works hard to expand the market for his catch. In their small town of La Push, there is little competition—with a single seafood buying company monopolizing the wharf. Dakwa sells the vast majority of his catch wholesale to this

"Our ancestors were fishermen, ocean-going people. We're just trying to pick up the first steps of our ancestors."

company, but has found innovative ways of bringing in other buyers from as far as Oregon and California.

His efforts to attract buyers help all the other local fishermen, both Native and non-Native, who receive better prices for their catch. Dakwa would like to buy his own semi and hopes one day to have a warehouse in Seattle. From there he could distribute his catch to farmers' markets and grocery stores where he could garner higher prices for his fresh seafood.

Dakwa donates great quantities of crab and fish to community events like potlatches, funerals, birthdays, and drumming ceremonies. Life is a community effort in La Push and Dakwa sees this giving as an opportunity to help strengthen his nation by providing healthy food for his people. "We gotta keep this stuff in our diet," he says. "Lots of the catch stays here in La Push."

Dakwa helps lead a weekly drumming ceremony in which community members bring potluck dishes to the local gym, hold a friendly supper, and then drum and sing traditional Quileute songs that echo along the shoreline. Dakwa tries to be a role model for younger people by supporting community activities like the drumming ceremonies.

"When I was young it wasn't cool to be traditional, but young kids see that I picked up the drum and they see success," he explains. "It's not all about roaming around on the rez and getting into alcohol and drugs."

Dakwa and his wife, Sandy, raise Shilaily to know her Quileute ways and also plan to raise their new baby boy traditionally. "We're gifted to still have a culture and heritage, so it's up to our younger generation to keep it alive," he says.

Dakwa and Sandy recently had a naming ceremony for the Seactis, where relatives and friends from as far as Canada journeyed for a night of ceremony and festivity. These ceremonies occur less and less nowadays, all the more reason for the Woodruffs to keep the tradition alive.

At age ten, Dakwa paddled for the Quileute in the first intertribal canoe gathering. Tribes all along the Washington coast carved and painted traditional cedar seafaring vessels and set off on the "Paddle to Seattle" in 1989. An amazing experience, Dakwa says, "After that first trip, I knew it was something I would take part in for the rest of my life."

Dakwa and his family support the canoe journeys as a way to join people together in a common task and honor their ancestors by holding traditional ceremonies with other Northwestern tribes. In the Woodruff's front yard sits a massive cedar tree trunk that they are carving into a thirty-foot traditional canoe. They will use it for the next intertribal canoe gathering to traverse the Pacific Ocean as their ancestors did for uncounted generations.

"When I was young it wasn't cool to be traditional, but young kids see that I picked up the drum and they see success."

Passionately Preserving Place

west virginia : hanna thurman

Since grade school, Hanna Thurman has been involved in everything from managing an ice cream shop to traditional dance and folklore preservation to activism against mountain top removal. Dedicated to her home state of West Virginia, she humbly shares the many accomplishments she has managed in just twenty-five years.

Raised in the small town of Liberty, Hannah credits her close family for her strong sense of place. "It's a very special place and always will be," she says. "I know very deeply what home is." For Hanna, home is about place, culture, nature, and the people she loves.

In grade school, Hanna made a name for herself as an Irish and Scottish dancer. She joined a dance group called the Appalachian Lads and Lassies, led by Jane George. Jane's spouse, Frank George, is a renowned fiddler and respected authority on West Virginian music history. Once sparked, her interest in dance took her traveling around the state to learn other traditional dances of Appalachia. Soon she was performing with groups across West Virginia.

In the summer of 2005, Hanna took part in Mountain Justice Summer in

"It's a very special place and always will be. I know very deeply what home is."

Naoma. The annual project brings together activists to build awareness about the effects of mountain top mining. That summer she worked with well-known activists from around the country. Her work included the Listening Project, where she went door-to-door to hear firsthand from residents how coal mining had affected residents' health and communities. Their goal was simply to get people thinking and talking about the effects of coal processing on the surrounding land and people.

That summer, Hanna also worked on a project in the community of Sundial, about thirty miles south of Charleston in the Coal River Valley. She fought to protect the students of Marsh Fork Elementary School, located four hundred yards downhill from one of Massey Energy Company's coal mining operations. Here billions of gallons of toxic sludge are held by an earthen dam. Similar dams have been known to breach, leading to some of the nation's worst environmental disasters.

Hanna passionately sums up the situation at the school. She says, "You run around in the playground and your feet are black from the coal dust!"

At one demonstration, Hanna traveled with a student's father to the energy company's headquarters in downtown Richmond to demand the closure of coal mining operations near the elementary school. Executives refused to meet with them. Hanna and the parent were determined not to leave without a guarantee the mining would be stopped. After three hours of waiting, they were arrested for trespassing—a fate that was common among nonviolent protesters demanding change from the coal company.

Looking back on the project, Hanna concedes that while they were never granted an opportunity to speak with executives, and more incidents continue to be documented, their work drew attention to the issues. She says, "One of the best things to come from the project is the relationships that have been formed between activists and community members. Some of the activists who had gone to the community to work on the project ended up permanently relocating there, so they could continue the battle against Massey and mountain top removal."

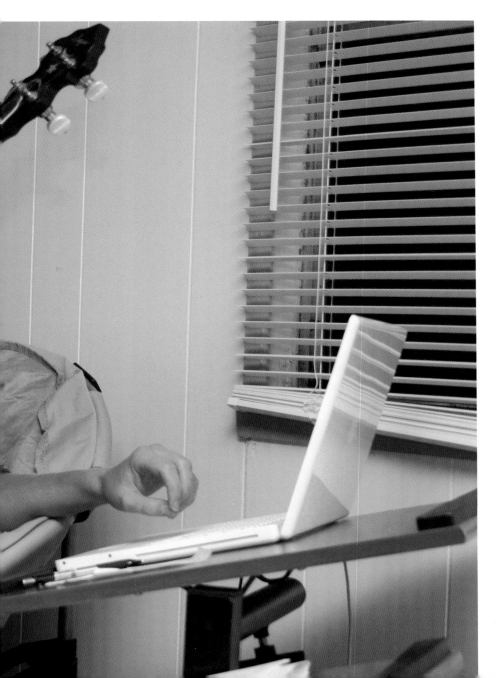

Hanna went on to work for the Preservation Alliance of West Virginia where she spent a year and a half working with the West Virginia Cultural Heritage Development Program conducting surveys. She smiles as she reflects on how much she enjoyed the job. "I got to travel between seven West Virginian communities to talk with the 'movers and shakers,'" she explains. "I was meeting the people who are really trying to create change. . . . I loved it!".

After her work with the Preservation Alliance, Hanna began thinking about what issues were especially important to her. The search to find an issue that deeply spoke to her brought Hanna back to her childhood passion: her love for traditional dance. That led her to Friends of Old Time Music and Dance (FOOTMAD).

Based in Charleston, FOOTMAD is the primary traditional dance and music organization in West Virginia. The volunteer-run organization was created in 1981 by a small group of individuals interested in tracing Appalachian sounds to their roots in Irish music. The organization soon broadened to include all forms of traditional music, blues, and bluegrass. FOOTMAD hosts various events—dances twice a month, six concerts a year, and an annual festival called the Fall Fling.

Hanna had been attending FOOTMAD dances since college, but later assumed a more central role as vice president of the organization. In this role, she organized volunteers, filed reports and wrote grants. In her year as vice president, Hanna worked diligently to involve young people because of her concern that so many young people are moving away from West Virginia.

Hanna moved to Morgantown in August of 2007 and is currently pursuing a masters in public administration and social work at West Virginia University. The change in location has only served to strengthen her passions. While she may not be able to take as active a role in FOOTMAD, folklore preservation, or fighting mountain top removal, she is now mobilizing the University's resources to broaden her horizons and to continue networking on these issues. Hanna still serves as a member of the FOOTMAD board, and, along with activists Michael and Carrie Kline, has recently recorded a CD.

Hanna dreams of one day creating her own business to work with families struggling to get their parents and grandparents into better situations as they age. "My goal," she says, "is to help the elderly feel like they've resolved their lives, so they won't be scared of leaving the world."

Regardless of where her new degrees lead her, Hanna will remain actively involved in music and dance and in working to alleviate the problems that plague her beloved homeland. She explains, "I feel a strong need to help this state. There's a lot of negative press associated with West Virginia. It's really time to do something positive."

"I got to travel between seven West Virginian communities to talk with the 'movers and shakers.' I was meeting the people who are really trying to create change. . . . I loved it!"

From Sun Dance to Community Plans

south dakota : nick tilsen

In late 2006, the pillars of a new ceremony house rose into the vast South Dakota sky, crafted by the hands of Lakota youth and families who had never built such a structure before. Medicine man Jerome Lebeaux, thirty, looked on with pride as his friends and members of the Thunder Valley Tiospaye (pronounced "tee-oh-sh-pie-ae") helped construct this community and ceremony house that has been long in the making. With little funding, but an abundance of helping hands, the building represents not just a new resource for young Lakota people on the Pine Ridge Indian Reservation, but also a leap of faith for the whole community.

A tiospaye is the most basic unit of Lakota society—the extended family network within a tribe that the U.S. Government tried hard to destroy. Tiospayes in Lakota country now slowly regenerate, like the American buffalo whose presence on the Great Plains grows stronger with each passing season. Lakota activist Nick Tilsen, twenty-six, recognizes strong links between the restoration of the Great Plains ecology and Lakota culture. While a traditional tiospaye includes only blood relations, in Thunder Valley a diversity of family, friends, and community members are united by a passion for rejuvenating Lakota culture.

The Lakota (or Sioux, as they and related tribes were named by their enemies) have a history of producing powerful spiritual and community leaders. From Black Elk and Fool's Crow to Chief Red Cloud and the legendary Crazy Horse, their descendants now struggle to rebuild a nation that was pushed to the brink of physical and spiritual destruction. Nick explains, "Rather than focus energy on what our government is not doing, we're focusing our energy on what we should be doing. We've decided as a community to take ownership of our own future." Ceremony by ceremony, project by project, prayer by prayer, they have made remarkable progress in recent years.

The ceremony house marked Nick's transition from leading the activism-based Lakota Action Network to joining with others to create the Thunder Valley Community Development Corporation (CDC), a nonprofit that will nurture a new generation of Lakota leaders. Throughout the last three years, rounds of community meetings and gatherings have kicked off an enthusiasm like never before, as the Thunder Valley Lakota take their future into their own hands and begin forming a twenty-year community development plan. The Thunder Valley CDC mission statement involves the words of over fifty Lakota youth and elders and aims to create a rebirth of traditional culture, values, and ceremonies that will offer youth the opportunity to build leadership skills—and stay away from drugs. Addressing social problems and planning for the future are especially critical on Pine Ridge, where more than half of the population is under twenty-four years old.

Now, the ceremony and community center brims with life five days a week hosting everything from sacred ceremonies and dances to baby showers and community suppers. A group of local mothers finally has space to organize and coach a modern hip-hop dance group of their daughters and other young women, called the Thunder Valley Dancing Divas. They have performed at major events across the reservation and South Dakota. A group of young men has formed a traditional drum group that performs both at public powwows and Lakota spiritual ceremonies.

Nick and Jerome have seen many important programs blossom from the community center such as the Youth Leadership Program, which coordinates mentoring in the schools, offers local leadership workshops, runs a sacred sites program, and provides a Lakota language program. Last year, twenty-five youth participated in ceremonies at the four sacred sites in the Black Hills (He Sapa in Lakota): Bear Butte, Harney Peak, Devils Tower, and Reynolds Prairie. This experience helped them learn firsthand about the power and importance of Lakota culture.

On the reservation, youth-led movements can be politically controversial because respect for elders is the cornerstone of Lakota ways. When Nick leans into the microphone at Pine Ridge's famous KILI radio station for a public service announcement, tradition dictates that he first respectfully ask permission to speak before his elders. Nick strives to honor the elders and explains that Thunder Valley CDC creates a vital space for elders to come share their wisdom and knowledge of Lakota ways with eager groups of youth.

Likewise, Jerome reveres all the elders and ancestors who have helped him become a medicine man and who instructed him in Lakota spiritual rites and ceremonies, since he was seven years old. His work would not be possible without these teachers. As a medicine man, Jerome devotes his life to the community, focusing especially on the youth. He sees great value in fostering spiritual growth in young people, and aims his efforts at teaching traditional Lakota ceremonies. He has had great success attracting young people to the ceremonies, as evidenced by strong youth participation in the annual Sun Dance. This ceremony is quintessential to Lakota spiritual ways and has endured despite generations of repression. When Jerome introduces

young Lakota to Inipi (sweat lodge) and other ceremonies, he does so to help them see who they are inside, develop pride in their culture, and reconnect with the power and guidance of their ancestors.

Recently, Thunder Valley CDC applied for and received a $300,000 grant from the federal government to plan a new type of community building that will house a much needed youth emergency shelter, community fitness center, and local business incubator. Remarkably, this grant earmarks money for land acquisition, enough to buy one hundred acres on which to house this facility.

Thunder Valley CDC plans to use this money to design the center and put a plan in place that will raise around one million dollars to construct and operate the center. Nick points out the urgent need for another youth crisis center on Pine Ridge. The average three-bedroom house currently has fourteen to fifteen occupants, and some youth and their families struggle with drug and alcohol abuse problems. Youth sometimes have to leave home, or have no home, and desperately need a safe place to receive emergency food, shelter, counseling, and referral to a cultural treatment program.

Thunder Valley CDC is also beginning to make a long-term community development plan that addresses economic, cultural, and ecological concerns. Nick says, "We want this community to be one of the greenest communities, not just in Indian Country, but in the whole United States. We are making huge strides to actually do it, not just talk about it."

Now, the ceremony and community center brims with life five days a week hosting everything from sacred ceremonies and dances to baby showers and community suppers.

Nick traces this spiritual and community renewal to when medicine man Jerome LeBeau and his family started a Sun Dance in Thunder Valley eleven years ago. Sun Dance is one of the most powerful and ancient ceremonies in which Lakota dancers worship in sweltering heat for four days with virtually no modern trappings, food, or water. Amidst drums, songs, and ceremonies with their families, the dancers praise the Creator and invoke the guidance of their ancestors with their suffering and devotion. Across Indian Country, and especially at Thunder Valley, Native youth are losing their fear or disdain of the Sun Dance and becoming inspired to learn the old ways. To be a Sun Dancer means returning to true Lakota values such as swearing off alcohol among other things. "People that make change in their own life want to see change in their communities," explains Nick.

The Sun Dance set the context in which Thunder Valley CDC could flourish with renewed youth enthusiasm and involvement. As the season for another Sun Dance approaches, more and more Lakota youth are working to rebuild the Lakota Nation one project, one ceremony, and one prayer at a time.

A Sustainable Catch

maine : john jordan

Lobstermen on Chebeague Island, near Portland, Maine, wake up early in the morning and spend much of the day checking traps marked by bright buoys dotting the glistening inlets of Casco Bay. Chebeague (pronounced "sheh-beeg" or "sheh-big" by locals) boasts a year round population of about three hundred fifty residents, but that figure balloons to more than two thousand in the summer when outsiders flock here to enjoy Maine's laid-back coastal beauty.

John Jordan, thirty-four, and his sternman Mark McGoon, twenty-nine, ply these chilly waters not just as independent lobstermen but as members of the newly formed Dropping Springs Lobster Cooperative. In the fiercely traditional lobstering culture, Dropping Springs presents a new sales and marketing option for lobstermen who sometimes stay loyal to one buyer for their entire lives.

John hails from the less-than-coastal state of Ohio, where his father was a college professor. Summers brought him and his family to Chebeague Island, where he experienced Maine's tight-knit communities and lobstering culture throughout his youth. John studied at Colby College in Maine, and in 1990, he started working as a sternman on a lobster boat where he helped a captain bait and haul traps. Whether it was the fresh air and freedom of working the seas, or the $120 a day he was earning for his backbreaking labor, this maritime trade worked its way into his blood.

After graduating from Colby, John applied for jobs on Wall Street, thinking his path lay among glowing computer screens in air-conditioned buildings. Despite the financial allure of a Wall Street career, he decided to return to Maine, trading stock ticker screens for sonar screens and the dangers of a lobster boat.

Maine's ruggedly independent lobstermen rarely share the secrets of their best yielding traps or the exact amounts of their catch. This tight lipped atmosphere allows wholesale buyers to set a low "boat price" for competing lobstermen, such that they earn about four dollars per pound, or less, for lobster that lands on plates at prices many times higher.

John helped found Dropping Spring Lobster Co-op in 2004 with nine other lobstermen. Their goal was to get higher prices via collective bargaining. In 2006, the co-op grew to nineteen members and had to buy lobster from nonmembers to fulfill

demand. John, who works as the co-op's manager, envisions opening a retail store nearby and driving a delivery truck to places like New Jersey, where the co-op's "boat price" could reach thirteen dollars per pound.

Lobsters, like lobstermen, are secretive and little understood. They can live for more than a hundred years and migrate many miles across the sea floor in trenches, usually going farther out in winters and crawling closer to shore in summertime. This tendency makes winter lobstering especially dangerous. Lobsters reach harvestable maturity by around seven to eight years, quite different from most livestock. Maine's lobster fishery self regulates with a vengeance, each lobsterman dutifully throwing back all breeding females and juveniles so the population remains sustainable and vibrant. A governing body sets trap limits according to zone. New lobstering licenses are about as easy to come by as an advanced medical degree.

John "fishes" eight hundred lobster traps, which he lays out in strings of eight or sixteen, marked by a buoy floating above each end of the submerged trap string. Each forty-pound metal trap may yield from zero to more than a dozen lobsters, depending on if it was well maintained, baited, positioned, and visited by lady luck. A winch hauls the heavy traps up from the sea floor at which time John and Mark rapidly pull lobsters out and measure them. If it's a keeper, they disable the lobster's powerful claws with a thick rubber band and store it in tanks on the boat. They then re-bait the trap with fish and heft it onto the boat's stern, where the re-baited string of traps will be jettisoned back into the water once the boat gets moving.

John comments, "One of the many dangers of lobstering involves getting entangled in the line connecting the weighted traps as they fly off the open back of the boat." Lobstering with a sternman not only improves productivity, but can also prevent fatal accidents. Having traversed the islands of Casco Bay countless times, John knows his boat and surroundings so intimately that in fog, he can navigate by how the sea floor looks on the sonar.

Each lobsterman paints their buoys in specific patterns, whether it be pink polka dots or a single stripe. Lobstermen pass the creative patterns down through generations. John's boat, the Katarina (named after his wife as tradition dictates) is thirty-four-feet long, sixteen-feet wide, and boasts two radars, sonar, GPS, and autopilot. It holds 300 gallons of diesel fuel for forays far out into rough water. The boat's small cabin and heater provide an essential cover from freezing rain and water during the bitterly cold months when, motivated by higher prices, lobstermen continue to operate.

Mark McGoon was born into lobstering on Chebeague and was on the boats by the time he was eight. He attended the Chebeague Island Elementary School, along with

In the fiercely traditional lobstering culture, Dropping Springs presents a new sales and marketing option for lobstermen who sometimes stay loyal to one buyer for their entire lives.

only thirty-two other students. Mark worked on the boats during high school, and after attending college for architectural drafting, he decided that his fate lay with lobstering. In 1998, he joined the Navy, forfeiting the lobstering license he had held for fifteen years. Upon his return from Iraq, he enrolled in Maine's lobsterman apprentice program and completed the required one thousand hours of boat time. That put him on the waiting list to get a license, which could mean a wait of as many as three years. "For every five retiring lobstermen, about one new license is granted," Mark explains.

John lives in the nearby mainland town of Yarmouth with his wife, Katarina, a primary school teacher. Mark also lives on the mainland, in the town of Gorham, with his wife. Like John, he was unable to afford the high property taxes levied on island homes. As Maine's coastal communities gentrify with the second homes of wealthy New Englanders, John fears for the fate of working waterfronts in Casco Bay.

Organizations like Dropping Springs may just help lobstermen maintain their place on the islands by guaranteeing that more money stays with the lobstermen and their crew. When Mark is eligible for a license again, he expects to join the co-op because it's simply a better business model. Each lobsterman (and the few lobsterwomen in the area) earns the same percentage that he or she catches. The co-op even divvies up a Christmas bonus to all its members based on profits.

Dropping Springs has a social element too, hosting an annual party for workers and their families. John plays harmonica and sings in a band called the Pollack (a type of fish) with a local member of the merchant marine and a worker from the bait shack where the co-op members go to unload lobster and refill bait. Performing, however, has taken a back seat with the addition of children to the family. And during the winter, when the Katarina may only go out once every two weeks, John drives a plow truck and digs eighty-seven clients out of their snow-filled driveways.

By logging long hours in some of the most physically and mentally challenging conditions possible, Maine lobstermen not only follow a time-honored tradition, but they also create one of the world's few truly sustainable fisheries. By organizing groups like Dropping Springs and promoting young lobstermen and women through the apprentice program, people like John Jordan and Mark McGoon hope to keep Casco Bay a working waterfront filled with lobstermen for many generations— and buoy pattern permutations— to come.

Organizations like Dropping Springs may just help lobstermen maintain their place on the islands by guaranteeing that more money stays with the lobstermen and their crew.

Ranching Poetic

nevada : kathi wines

Imagine a small rural community in northeastern Nevada. The air is thick with the smell of sagebrush, and beautiful aspen and willow trees provide shade for passersby. Visitors may look up and find themselves staring in wonder at the Ruby Mountains. Yet behind these sights and smells lies an old and important tradition: ranching. Such is Lamoille, Nevada. Traditionally a prosperous ranching community, this area, as well as its famous Lamoille Canyon, attracts visitors from near and far.

As populations grows in this region, so do competing land pressures. "People are discovering that land is worth more money as real estate than as ranching land," says Kathi Wines, a fourth generation rancher from Lamoille. "They don't understand that if we keep going in this direction, we'll be importing all of our food. We'll also lose the unique ranching heritage that makes up the American West."

Kathi is dedicated to preserving this cultural heritage. "What makes northeastern Nevada so special is the tradition it holds true to," she explains. One effort she works on is the National Cowboy Poetry Gathering, which takes place every January at the Western Folklife Center in Elko, about twenty miles from Lamoille. Kathi helps organize this event that draws people from across the U.S. and around the world. The gathering celebrates life in the rural West through contemporary and traditional arts, including music, poetry readings, and storytelling.

In addition to this event, Kathi works year round to share her culture with others and educate them on the ranching lifestyle of the past, as well as the present. She knows some information circulated about ranchers puts them in a bad light, and wants to make sure that her side of the story gets told.

Born and raised in Lamoille on her family's ranch, Kathi grew up riding horses and tending to baby calves. "It's a pretty unique bond with nature. That's where my heart is," Kathi says.

Her love for her community was nurtured in 4-H and Future Farmers of America (FFA). On the ranch, Kathi loves helping irrigate the meadows in the spring and summer, and cutting down the hay in July—a tradition she has taken part in ever since she was eleven years old. According to Kathi, many chores haven't changed throughout the years, though technology has made it much easier for both ranchers and cattle.

"When I'm trotting my horse on a circle looking for cows on our summer range," Kathi says, "I can't help but think that this may be the same path my grandfather took when he rode looking for his cows years ago. And I hope someday to have a grandchild who will ride this path in fifty or sixty years looking for her cows."

Kathi and her family raise commercial crossbreed Black Angus cows. The day-to-day routine is constantly changing. In the spring the calves are born, branded, and vaccinated against disease. A time of togetherness, friends, family, and neighbors all come out to get the work done.

By late April, the cows are turned out in the summer range, comprised of federal land allotted to the family for grazing. The area offers large expanses of sagebrush and native grasses. Then, in mid-May, the cows are bred to the bulls.

After the hay gathering is complete, the cattle are brought back to the pastures. Many of the calves are sold and shipped off in late October, weighing between 400 and 600 pounds. Those that remain are weaned in November, and the whole herd is fed throughout the winter before the cycle starts again in the spring.

Kathi attended the University of Nevada-Reno where she majored in journalism with an emphasis on public relations. Now back in Lamoille, she serves as president of the Elko County Cattlewomen. This is another venue for educating the public about ranching culture and the beef industry. Among other things, the group does cooking demonstrations in grocery stores and presentations to school children. Kathi likes visiting with kids and talking to them about the food they eat. She says, "It's kind of scary when kids think their food comes from the grocery store."

Kathi attributes much of her success to her family and to people at the Western Folklife Center. The most challenging part of her work is combating misinformation. There has always been some tension between environmentalists, animal rights activists, and ranchers. By getting the right information out, Kathi feels she has been successful in persuading people that ranching is important to America's culture. "If I convince one person, it's worth it," she says. "That is one person that goes home and has more respect for ranching and the people who are doing it."

The ranch has taught Kathi responsibility, the importance of family, integrity, and the reality of life and death. She has learned to love nature, and respect the animals that provide her livelihood. Kathi treasures the rural life, and cherishes the memories and values it has instilled in her. Deeply rooted in this area, she has no plans to leave.

"The younger generations will determine the future of ranching," she says. So to foster their interest, she helps with the local 4-H club and participates in her old FFA chapter. She also helps organize the Elko County Fair.

"The truth is, everything in ranching is about the kids," Kathi says. She hopes to be blessed with children of her own, and envisions a ranching future with them: horses just outside their backdoor and 4-H steers in the barn. With this dream in mind, and a passion for what she does in her heart, Kathi will continue to renew her rural community.

four : toward a healthy planet

The natural world defines the heart of the countryside. From the Colorado River to Upstate New York, and off the back roads of every state across the country, our homeland harbors an extraordinary wealth of natural beauty.

As urbanization swallows acre after acre of land, and much of our countryside is paved over with parking lots or transformed into monocultures, we need brave, smart young people on the job. We need a corps of people who will stand up to forces bent on shortsighted, short-term gains; people who can envision smart and sustainable solutions.

In this chapter, we visit a few of these young people who are working to preserve, protect, and carefully utilize the gifts of our natural world. From a group of college friends who run a thriving wind power business in New York, to a young North Dakota woman fostering organic farming in the Great Plains, these are stories that inspire.

With most of our precious natural resources located in rural areas, we need good stewards on the land ensuring their healthy future. Whether creating eco-friendly businesses or working for organizations and agencies, we need people like those showcased here, people who understand that the very health of our human race is intimately entwined with the natural environment.

Hometown Horticulture

massachusetts : raina webber

Just five years ago Raina Webber, twenty-five, rarely saw native plants alongside the byways of rural Housatonic, in the Berkshires of Massachusetts. Today, the natives are making a strong comeback. This revitalization is in part due to Project Native, a nonprofit group Raina founded in 2000, when she was just nineteen. The new native abundance also arises from her occasional "seed bombs," distributed Johnny Appleseed style from a moving car window.

Project Native grows indigenous plants in the Berkshire Taconic region and sells them to homeowners, landscapers, and institutions. Collecting the precious seed lines of genetic variations that evolved locally for thousands of years requires one of Raina's favorite activities: hiking. She explains, "In the early years, I would spend lots of time hiking, canoeing, and roaming over old railroad beds and logging trails, crisscrossing the rugged Berkshire terrain in search of surviving native plants."

Project Native has grown from just one-eighth of an acre—as an arm of The Railroad Street Youth Project—to forming its own nonprofit in 2003. They now have a farm of 150 acres where they cultivate a myriad of native plant species previously forgotten by all but local botany enthusiasts.

Raina inspires those around her with a vast knowledge of native plants and bright enthusiasm to address new challenges. "I earned straight As in high school, but got frustrated and bored with formal education, so I dropped out," says Raina, (though she doesn't recommend this to others). She traveled to Hawaii after her sixteenth birthday and began learning about permaculture and the importance of native plants to their ecosystems. In Hawaii, she made a living by growing and selling fruit trees and credits this work as her first experience with professional horticulture.

When she returned to the mainland and began working as a gardener, she attended a Nature Conservancy conference on native plants. "I was shocked to hear 500 participants lamenting the lack of native plant nurseries in Massachusetts," she says. Most native nurseries dealt with plants native to the entire U.S. or large multi-state regions. Berkshire landscapers were mail-ordering rarer varieties of native plants, thus ignoring the genetic lines that evolved just miles away in the Berkshires' wooded valleys and hillsides.

Project Native currently grows more than 130 varieties of native plants using exclusively organic methods. Most plants came from local seeds collected from private landowners, state parks, marshes, and public lands. Raina now has two full-time and three part-time employees, along with a host of volunteers. Eager workers come not only to revive native plants, but also to work outside with their hands in a culture that increasingly promotes indoor careers.

Raina began Project Native through grant funding, but now grants only make up a third of the revenue. Plant sales and individual donations make up the rest, and plant sales are on the rise. Now with a farm store, tours, a newsletter to donors, and more institutional clients, Project Native's outlook is diversifying, and thereby growing more financially sustainable.

"Propagating native plants is hard work," Raina explains, "because they often grow slower than invasive, hybridized, or genetically engineered plants." Project Native's

Project Native now has a farm of 150 acres where they cultivate a myriad of native plant species previously forgotten by all but local botany enthusiasts.

organic, low-fertilizer philosophy not only improves human health and minimizes environmental impacts, but it also serves the plants well. They adapt to survive in the wild without pesticides or synthetic fertilizers, thus they can be easily reintroduced to the countryside.

A curiosity about Berkshire native plants unites Project Native employees. The workers gather for weekly weeding days and Friday meetings. Smiling, Raina explains that the meetings always run too long because everyone has stories to share about the past week's plantings.

"I really encourage self-motivation here," she says. "If you have an idea of something that should get done, run it by me. It's rare that I won't agree to it."

Project Native's sales usually go to one of three major constituencies: homeowners, landscaping companies, and institutions. Raina laments that renters often lack the incentive to improve the long-term plant communities around their rented abodes. The group recently finished their largest project, a wetland restoration on an old airstrip that covered more than six acres. They've also done native plant restoration and gardening for nearby colleges, museums, businesses, and other institutions.

Raina and company open the plant nursery and grounds to a variety of visiting groups: from three-week summer camp, where participants learn about wild edible plants, to boarding school students, Girl Scouts, and others who want to learn about their hometown horticultural heritage. "I hope to remodel our ancient barn into a large educational center," says Raina. This and other projects are now being written into their ten-year plan. As the knotted Berkshire hills regain some of their threatened native species, so grows Project Native with Raina and a host of others at the horticultural helm.

As the knotted Berkshire hills regain some of their threatened native species, so grows Project Native with Raina and a host of others at the horticultural helm.

Wind Powers Friendship

new york : kevin schulte

Kevin Schulte, thirty, looks up with an impish smile. He's in the middle of a botched attempt to set up an A-frame tent when he exclaims boisterously, "Building wind turbines is a lot easier!"

He throws the poles down; it's time for a work break. He's been at it for a while in preparation for Sustainable Energy Developments' (SED) annual Labor Day Extravaganza. Every fall, friends and family come from far and wide to "let their hair down" and enjoy life together at the company farm. Yes, the company farm. This is not your typical company picnic, and SED is not your typical company. Only two of the eighteen employees are over thirty, yet they've signed millions of dollars worth of wind turbine contracts. Senior Project Manager Dave Strong explains that SED succeeds not because of one or two visionary leaders, but by working together. "SED is nothing without everybody," he says.

Kevin majored in integrated science and technology with concentrations in energy and the environment at James Madison University. He studied wind energy in Malta, and learned about European wind energy markets with his two friends Scott Abbett and Loren Pruskowski. The three joined forces to write their senior thesis, a plan for a 65 megawatt wind farm in West Virginia. After college, the friends went off to work in different aspects of the the wind industry—Kevin traveling to Texas to work on industrial scale turbine projects and Loren to upstate New York.

On a September morning in Austin, Texas, Kevin received a phone call from Loren. "Hey, are you ready to start a wind company with me?" Loren asked.

In the past two years, Kevin had helped construct around 600 megawatts worth of wind energy and his friend's proposition came at an ideal time. Kevin made a snap decision and dove in all the way. "Yeah, definitely man," he replied.

He soon quit his high-paying wind energy consulting job, wrapped up his Texas affairs, and drove to upstate New York to start a business with some of his best friends. Despite the prevailing sentiment that one should avoid starting a business with friends, Kevin urges everyone to do exactly that—launch innovative endeavors with the people you know and trust.

SED began with five college friends living together in a crowded one-bedroom apartment in Schenectady, New York. They established a nightly rotation where people shifted from the air mattress, to the bed, to the couch. Luckily the company's headquarters only remained so cramped for six weeks, after which they moved to Delanson, New York where the company grew for three and a half years.

They yearned for access to a metro area, but still wanted to remain rural. Finally, an innovative green entrepreneur, Bob Bechtold, offered them a renewably-powered office facility connected to his new biodiesel plant.

The turbines that SED installs differ philosophically from many of the large wind projects catapulting up across the U.S. Their projects focus on offsetting electricity costs for everything from individual families, to schools, to institutions, to businesses. By encouraging people to build individual turbines in areas where the human footprint has already transformed the landscape, SED's projects meet less resistance from environmental lobbies. Their largest project to date, the first ever wind turbine at a ski resort, didn't disturb a single tree, and stands in an area where the mountain has already been permanently altered. With annual snowfall dwindling at most ski resorts, owners have often been forced to consume massive electrical loads making artificial snow, and ironically, contributing even further to the climate crisis that plagues skiers and their beloved snow. At Jiminy Peak in western Massachusetts, they are now generating 33 to 50 percent of their own electrical needs with their turbine, and are working to reverse this vicious cycle.

The crew recently installed a large turbine for a local high school. The wind generator will save the school at least $150,000 in energy costs, which SED estimates should cover two annual teachers' salaries plus textbooks and more. The turbine is expected to meet 100 percent of the school's energy needs. SED lobbies New York State to consider these turbines capital improvements, as they have the potential to reduce school costs and the cumbersome state education budget. The business strives to combine sound economics with public education not just through marketing to schools, but by spending extensive time and energy informing people about wind power and explaining the nuts and bolts of energy dynamics in plain language.

When asked where he pictures the company in ten years, Kevin Schulte can only smile. It will remain one in which people treat each other as friends, and one which is lead by a solid vision of enhancing community spirit both inside the company and with all its partners. The SED crew works in a market gap. When most companies focus

on enormous wind farms of 10 to 1000 megawatts or specialize in single home turbines of around 10 kilowatts, SED focuses on medium-sized projects to power businesses and institutions. The company has three main branches: feasibility (which studies wind potential at sites), design, and construction. By focusing on "distributed generation," SED helps businesses and institutions to generate much or all of their own power and be semi-independent from the grid.

The SED projects generally remain connected to the power grid, using it like a backup battery. In times of strong wind and low demand, the turbines contribute extra energy into the grid. In this way the turbine runs the client's energy meter backwards, and allows the owner to receive payment in accordance with the given state's "net metering" laws and whatever contract the turbine owners may have with their local utility. In times of low wind and high demand, a facility can also draw power from the grid to supplement the turbine.

SED plans each turbine to offset that facility's annual energy usage while providing a steady and secure flow of electricity in times of moderate to strong wind. Today's turbines generate power on even slower wind speeds than ever before, thus enhancing the turbine's usefulness.

The SED crew wanted to establish deeper roots in their new community, so five of them decided to buy an overgrown, run-down farm in nearby Sodus, just a mile from the shores of Lake Ontario. Over the course of a year, they've reclaimed the farm, tended its eighty apple trees, installed a cider press, a beautiful stone smokehouse, and a chicken coop. They've also converted the old barn to a tool shed serious enough for five young, technically-minded tinkerers. After much hard work, their lush garden is blooming and provides all of the vegetables they need. A site is marked where a new prototype wind turbine will be built, only the second of its kind. Dense woods conceal a lively stream and trails lead to an open field where the stage and cordwood bar are set for the Labor Day Extravaganza.

The two-day festival is not just a big party with campfires and live music; it's like a family reunion. SED, more than almost any company of its size, is truly like a family. Although everyone has a different role to fulfill, nobody is made to feel superior or inferior as they join forces to hoist aloft the machines that help make clean, homegrown energy a reality.

Despite the prevailing sentiment that one should avoid starting a business with friends, Kevin urges everyone to do exactly that—launch innovative endeavors with the people you know and trust.

Organic Farming 101

north dakota : britt jacobson

Britt Jacobson is running ten minutes late, a very out-of-the-ordinary fact. She is driving west across North Dakota. It's an hour's drive from her house in Valley City to her office in Medina. She knows these roads like the lines on the palm of her hand. Britt grew up north of here, on an organic farm fifteen miles south of Canada. She went to college to the east, across the river from Fargo.

Every summer, Britt and her husband drive west to the North Dakota Badlands. She jokes that North Dakota feels like a really big town with a spread-out population. "It's not six degrees of separation," she laughs, "it's more like two and a half."

With 635,000 people, North Dakota is the third-least-populated state in the country, and it's a state in flux.

"It used to be east versus west in North Dakota, but more and more, it's urban versus rural," Britt says. "The numbers in urban places have been rising. But I don't know a single small town that isn't losing population."

Consider Medina, home to four churches, two bars and 312 people. In cities, grass and trees can feel like afterthoughts, fighting an uphill battle against roads and buildings. But in Medina, farmland dominates; some of the roads aren't paved. If development is a war between the natural earth and human invention, in Medina the earth is winning.

On a downtown corner stands the Decoy Bar. It shares a building with the Coffee Cup, which is only open part-time. Next door is Medina Drug, its door locked and yellow paper taped inside the window. Then there's the Medina Fire Hall, a two-story building that doubles as the visitor's information center, the Medina City Offices, the

Amadou started his proverbial walk into the woods in Senegal, where he grew up. He studied agricultural science in Tunisia, and completed his first master's degree in animal science. After a few years back home running the family business, he went to Tuskegee University in Alabama for a second master's, this time in agricultural and resource economics. Along the way, he's picked up a remarkable array of languages including: Wolof, Pular, French, Spanish, Arabic, and English. If only a few of those come in handy in the rural South, his other skills, luckily, come in multiples as well.

Based in Atlanta, Georgia, Amadou works for the Federation of Southern Cooperatives. The Federation, born out of the civil rights movement, is a nonprofit that strives to help black and other underserved farmers stay on their land by setting up cooperatives, teaching sustainable agriculture, promoting silvopasture, setting up credit unions, assisting with marketing, and running a youth development program. They also run a workforce development program, teaching members how to type, get a GED, build a résumé, and take online classes. The Federation has offices in four southern states and about two thousand members spanning thirteen states.

Amadou, for his part, directs the Black Belt Legacy Forestry Program.

"Much of southern land, now that no one's left to work it, is planted fencepost-to-fencepost with cheap, short-rotation loblolly pines that get clear-cut every twenty or thirty-five years," he explains. "A lot of farmers are unaware of their rights, the value of their land, or other things they might do with it."

Farmers with small acreages, especially those who just want to thin their forests rather than clear-cut, can't find people willing to cut their trees for a fair price. In short, brainstorming other roles for forested land has begun to look like a better and better idea. Amadou visits landowners who call the Federation requesting a consultant and works with them to develop ways to add value to their forests.

One example that shows promise in Georgia is silvopasture, or combining forestry and grazing on the same acreage—providing landowners with both short- and long-term income opportunities. While cows need grass to eat, goats thrive on the variety of undergrowth in forests. Goat manure fertilizes the trees, and their voracious appetites help keep the ground clear of underbrush, reducing the need to burn—a common practice in conventional tree farming that's not always feasible. In Georgia and elsewhere in the South, an increasing demand for goat meat, especially in ethnic markets, has made this a legitimate and profitable addition to silvopasture.

"The aim is to be equally sustainable in terms of the people, the environment, and economics," Amadou explains. "Don't just export your wood, keep the profit in the community. Create a local industry like floor or furniture making. Get a portable sawmill."

Amadou believes that even if growing longleaf pine or hardwood takes longer, the benefits are multifaceted; the biodiversity and economic potential in these forests is outstanding. He explains, "Short rotation pine forests for pulpwood are fast, easy money, which is why many people in Georgia have chosen that option, but we're not just

"The aim is to be equally sustainable in terms of the people, the environment, and economics. . . . Don't just export your wood: Keep the profit in the community."

appealing to sentiment when we recommend native hardwood and longleaf pine forests for lumber instead." They make financial sense, too. The quail, deer, and raccoon come back, and recreation is a growing sector, so people can offer hunting, hiking, or horseback riding on their land, another added income possibility.

Recently, Amadou began working with the National Wildlife Foundation in Atlanta on their national Longleaf Pine Restoration campaign. "The longleaf pine ecosystem is a unique working forest where timber production, game management, and biodiversity conservation are compatible and mutually beneficial," he says.

Amadou also participates in running the youth development program, bringing ten to fifteen local teenagers together each summer to learn about soil, growing food, and selling at the farmers' market. More importantly, the program teaches young people valuable skills: the art of running a business, marketing, sales techniques.

"The first weekend at the farmers' market, they sold nothing," says Amadou. "They were very upset. I said, 'Develop your social skills! Market your produce!' We talked about it. Eventually, they sold out."

Even though the American South is miles away—both geographically and culturally—from Amadou's home in Senegal, he loves the forest, the people, and the Federation as if he were born and raised here.

"Rural communities still have the values that have vanished from most cities," says Amadou. "They remind me of home a little bit."

While the Federation aims to help minority and underserved farmers, employees like Amadou make their services available to everyone. "If you're a small farmer in a rural community, you're struggling whether you're black or white, young or old," Amadou points out. But in this corner of Georgia, step-by-step against escalating odds, Amadou Diop is working to change that.

Protecting Public Lands

wyoming : lisa dardy mcgee

Growing up in Ohio, Lisa Dardy McGee had always wanted to travel and see the West. "My family wasn't outdoorsy. I had never camped or backpacked until I was in college," she says. "Then, in my sophomore year, I learned about summer internships and jobs in parks and forests."

While scooping ice cream in Grand Canyon National Park wasn't exactly what she envisioned, the job opened her eyes to new landscapes and potential careers. Currently the director of the National Parks and Forests Program for the Wyoming Outdoor Council, that first job now seems like a serendipitous beginning to a love affair with public lands.

Lisa went back to school after her first summer season, exploring her interests in art history, anthropology, and women's studies, but her enthusiasm for public lands was cemented. Another summer would see Lisa acting as a naturalist in Yellowstone National Park at the famous geyser, Old Faithful.

After college, Lisa became a seasonal park ranger in Grand Teton National Park, where she lived for four years in the small town of Kelly, Wyoming, and eventually met her husband, Matthew. The mountains of Wyoming were a large part of what drew her to stay.

"I fell in love with the Tetons," she says. "I loved living in a place where a moose in your front yard was a valid excuse for being late for work."

Being a federal employee had its ups and downs. "I learned that the Forest Service and the National Park Service were often under pressure to implement ill-conceived projects that had nothing to do with protecting natural resources," says Lisa.

Lisa took an internship at the Jackson Hole Conservation Alliance, working as an outreach assistant for the organization. In this position—her first with a nonprofit—she realized that her interest was in working with the issues directly, rather than organizing events.

"Within many environmental advocacy groups," says Lisa, "it seemed the people who dealt with the issues were lawyers or scientists. I knew I needed to go back to school to be effective in an advocacy role."

Back to school it was—this time for a law degree. Lisa studied public land law and natural resources law at the University of Wyoming College of Law in Laramie. She spent a year clerking for a judge in Alaska after graduation. Lisa is licensed in both Alaska and Wyoming. Though she is not litigating, she says the foundation in law is indispensable to her work.

"The Wyoming Outdoor Council was founded in 1967 to protect Wyoming's environment and quality of life for future generations," Lisa explains.

Her position puts her directly between the public and those who create and implement public land policy. Typically, in Wyoming, those policies involve management decisions regarding oil and gas development, logging, protecting roadless forest areas, and other uses of public lands.

Lisa works with federal agencies, elected officials, citizens, and other conservation organizations, helps coordinate outreach events, and determines ways to best mobilize the public.

By and large, the political climate of Wyoming is not friendly to "environmental" types, but its citizens do value their vast public lands, and fiercely. The trick is finding ways to

get their support, as organizations like the Wyoming Outdoor Council often carry a stigma with certain constituencies. "Recently, we've been working with outfitters, ranchers, and hunters to help us reach our elected officials," Lisa says.

Wyoming is a conservative state, but the town of Lander seems to embody an emerging new population. "Lander is quite progressive for Wyoming," says Lisa, now thirty-four. Home to several nonprofits, like the state seat of the Nature Conservancy and the international headquarters of the National Outdoor Leadership School (NOLS), the population of the area is a blend of outdoor adventure-seeking transplants, third and fourth generation ranchers, and members of the Shoshone and Arapaho tribes on the nearby Wind River Indian Reservation.

"In Lander, I feel like I'm part of a community that cares about social and environmental issues," Lisa says. "But there are a lot of people, even in Lander, who disagree with the work the Council does."

Lisa manages the Wyoming Outdoor Council's involvement with several programs—all focused on federal lands. Her job can find her on a conference call about issues affecting the Greater Yellowstone ecosystem in the morning and drafting a response to an Environmental Impact Statement in the afternoon.

"In this line of work, the timeline by which we measure success can be vast," she says. "A campaign might last five to ten years and we often consider a 'win' a retention of what we already have—in other words, keeping wild places the way they are now."

Although seeing the "end of the tunnel" on a given project can be a challenge, the small victories along the way can be extremely gratifying for Lisa and her colleagues. Just this year she filed an appeal that stopped the development of new oil and gas wells in the Wyoming Range—a beloved part of the Bridger-Teton National Forest south of Jackson Hole.

Public dialogue and debate is critical to the work of the Wyoming Outdoor Council. "We've worked closely with citizens to protect the Wyoming Range," says Lisa. When she's on the road, it's not infrequent for her to meet with biologists and ATV enthusiasts in the same day. She adds, "We always ask ourselves how we can reach out to new groups of people."

It's not only the sociopolitical landscape that Lisa finds to be fertile ground for her work. "I have a sense of place here that I don't think I'd experience anywhere else," she says. "Although there are a lot of great conservation organizations in larger cities, I don't think I'd feel as connected to the land in a place like Denver, for example. In Lander, the mountains are in my backyard and my commute to work is a four-block walk."

"Although there are a lot of great conservation organizations in larger cities, I don't think I'd feel as connected to the land in a place like Denver, for example. In Lander, the mountains are in my backyard and my commute to work is a four block walk."

Small-town life is conducive to a career in public service. "When you work for a nonprofit organization, it helps to live in an affordable place," says Lisa. "My job's flexibility and benefits also make up for what it might lack in pay."

While she may not have envisioned the path to her current job that first summer in the Grand Canyon, Lisa is grateful for the end result. "I feel very lucky to have this job," she says. "I'm in the position that I wanted to be in all along."

five : food for thought

Today, eighty percent of Americans live in urban centers. Connections to our agrarian roots and food traditions have severely deteriorated. In the last half of the twentieth century, we were swept into an increasingly industrial food system that promised convenience and cheap food. The average distance from farm to table grew to over a thousand miles and processed food became king.

But a local foods movement, that has quietly been brewing for many years, has mushroomed in the twenty-first century. People are hungry to know where their food comes from and eager to prepare and savor real food. From Community Supported Agriculture (CSA), to farmers' markets, to community gardens, to more local products in grocery stores, producers and consumers alike are finding ways to support and grow a new model for food production.

In this chapter, we visit some of the people who are making a difference in their communities by offering local, sustainable, and healthy foods. We visit a young philosopher raising and marketing heritage breeds of livestock; a third-generation butcher preparing top quality meats for his community; two families producing an array of amazing dairy products; and a winemaker in the Heartland.

From the Louisville lambs, who are learning to be savvy gardeners at a very young age, to a group of students running a farm on campus, this chapter is full of examples of how people across the country are re-creating the lost local food system. It is a taste of the nation.

A Thinking Man's Abode

arkansas : ragan sutterfield

Ragan Sutterfield embodies unexpected juxtapositions: birdwatcher and blogger, poststructuralist theory enthusiast and pig farmer, agrarian thinker and activist. He leases land from a Berkeley astrophysicist. Thus you might be surprised to find Ragan living happily in Morrilton, Arkansas.

Morrilton, about an hour northwest of Little Rock, is emphatically not a hippie enclave in the mold of Asheville or Missoula. The road signs are ridden with bullet holes and illegal cock fighting abounds. There's only one grass-finished, Wendell Berry-spouting farmer and animal breeder for miles around, and it's Ragan.

In high school, when Ragan and a few of his friends would get together at the Waffle House, they'd discuss philosophy. Reading John Dewey even inspired them to write a manifesto against education. They all left Arkansas for college, but nearly all of them have—or plan to—come back.

"In high school I developed the communitarian ideal," Ragan says, "but it wasn't until college, when I started reading Berry and Wes Jackson and what they'd written about becoming native to a place, that I started considering farming."

Ragan graduated in 2002 from Wheaton with a degree in philosophy. Returning to Morrilton, Ragan apprenticed with a local Katahdin Hair Sheep breeder, Ed Martsolf, something of a farming celebrity himself. A year's worth of work earned him a small flock of lambs, which he sold to local restaurants and farmers' markets. He added some pigs—Gloucester Old Spots, a breed threatened with extinction because they did not thrive in pens, but "mighty tasty," says Ragan. He built up a small herd by virtue of his two bristly, mean-looking boars, who answer to the names Plato and Aristotle.

Next, Ragan acquired a few Charolais-Angus beef cows, and most recently, he started a Chicken Club, where people pay $175 and receive sixteen chickens over four months. He sells the eggs from his 300 free-range laying hens. His leased land covers eighty acres, plenty of space for several hundred animals.

"I want my farm to be market-driven and independent," Ragan says. This has required some creative financing.

"As a young farmer, you can't get a loan to do anything interesting," Ragan explains. "The only money you can get is for row crops and cow/calf operations, both of which are heavily subsidized. I hate subsidies."

So far, Ragan has bought only animals, based on his experience that buying land is a tremendous burden on young farmers, and leasing has been cheaper than the interest on a mortgage. He cites an Amish saying, "Build the barn before you buy the house," explaining that once the farm is set up, he plans on purchasing acreage. His investment in equipment has been minimal, too—an old farm truck with more than 250,000 miles and an ancient tractor.

"Plato and Aristotle can dig a four-by-three foot pit in no time," says Ragan, "so I've been thinking about using the pigs to replace my tractor. Why use technology when the animals are happy to do the work?"

Farming isn't Ragan's only occupation. He spends about half his time writing: a blog on *Plenty* magazine's website, book reviews for the *Arkansas Democrat-Gazette*, an article on heritage pork for *Men's Journal*, and a piece on what to know about your farmer for *Gourmet* magazine. He's got a book in the works on agrarian philosophy. An avid reader, on any day you can find Ragan engrossed in *The Stockman Grass Farmer*, *Acres USA*, *The New Yorker*, *Farming* magazine, *Arts & Letters Daily*, a Faulkner novel or Michael Pollan's latest work. He occasionally teaches a class (on Zizek and the philosopher Alain Badiou) at a local college, and can hold his own on the likes of Noam Chomsky, Jacques Lacan, or Alasdair MacIntyre.

"In high school I developed the communitarian ideal, but it wasn't until college, when I started reading Berry and Wes Jackson and what they'd written about becoming native to a place, that I started considering farming."

A typical day for Ragan starts around 4 a.m. After a breakfast of farm eggs and Old Spot sausages, he writes for a few hours. Days are busy—checking on the animals, mending fences, washing and carting eggs, making deliveries to Little Rock, and checking on the animals again before bed, many hours later.

"NPR is my companion," he jokes. "I've gotten to know all the reporters *real* well."

"When people who knew me in high school see me back in town, they ask me what happened. They figure something must've gone wrong. They can't imagine that someone who left would come back to farm," says Ragan. "These days, people go looking for opportunities rather than creating them at home, so rural areas just get brain-drained."

Farming, he explains, has gone through some difficult times in Arkansas. After one of the state's largest agribusinesses drastically lowered prices, many small pig farmers went out of business.

"Thankfully, I'm not trying to compete with the Tyson's of this world," he says.

Hoping to create some of those "opportunities" that will attract other bright young people to the state, Ragan chairs the board of an interest group that worked to create a Department of Agriculture for the state, which lacked one until recently.

Ragan believes his future lies in heritage breeds, like his Gloucester Old Spots. "The factory food industry has figured out how to do organic," he notes, "and they're working on figuring out how to do local. But it's impossible to farm heritage-breed animals or heirloom vegetables on a massive scale. I think heritage breeds are where people will look next for authenticity in their food."

That's where farmers' markets come in.

"The farmers' market, fortunately, opens me up to a whole different group of people," he says.

Like other local growers, Ragan is finding plenty of outlets for his products. In nearby Little Rock, he makes deliveries to Imagine, a recently opened restaurant that sources nearly all of its produce and meat from Arkansas farmers, and to Hardin's Mercantile in the River Market District, run by Jody Hardin, a fifth-generation Arkansas farmer, who sells his own and other local goods.

Says Jody, "My lease agreement specifies that I have to sell popular items like bananas, tomatoes, avocados, pineapples, and oranges beside the rest of my merchandise, but in a year we've accumulated 180 CSA (Community Supported Agriculture) members, and the baskets are doing real well."

November's basket includes spinach, turnip greens, spaghetti and acorn squash, pecans, Arkansas black apples, short-grain brown Arkansas rice, sweet potatoes, fresh pasta made with Ragan's eggs, and a gorgeous Adama chicken. No one misses the bananas.

The rising demand for local foods gets Ragan's juices flowing. Future plans include setting up a dairy for cheese making with heritage-breed cows, and pairing up

"When people who knew me in high school see me back in town, they ask me what happened. They figure something must've gone wrong. They can't imagine that someone who left would come back ... to farm. These days, people go looking for opportunities rather than creating them at home, so rural areas just get brain drained."

with a vegetable farmer to create CSA baskets. A current project involves expanding his charcuterie (an ancient European meat preservation technique) offerings. Assisted by a chef at the Boulevard Bakery in Little Rock, Ragan is experimenting with recipes for Arkansas prosciutto.

"Our very scientific technique?" jokes the chef: "Two hams require the weight of six heavy cans of pork-and-beans, for as long as necessary until they feel ready to the touch."

Smoking and curing more meat, and offering a CSA meat box are also on Ragan's "to-do" list.

This Arkansas-kid-gone-thinking man remains highly susceptible to the written word. After reading Thoreau's quote, "Water is the only drink for a wise man. Wine is not a noble liquor; and think of dashing the hopes of a morning with a cup of warm coffee, or of an evening with a dish of tea," Ragan drank only water for a year. But if his head is sometimes in the clouds, his feet are planted firmly on Arkansas soil.

"Farming is romantic like marriage is romantic," says Ragan. "Sometimes it is. Sometimes it isn't."

Respect for New Sprouts

mississippi : louisville lambs

The Winston County Self-Help Cooperative meets three or four times a week at the Mount Moriah Baptist Church, in Louisville, Mississippi. Its twenty-one members sit in folding metal chairs waiting for the meeting to begin. "Sit" is a misnomer. They writhe. They batter each other across the table. Some of the older girls practice elegant and elaborate disaffection, while the boys make faces at one another. The Co-op members, children ages five to eighteen, are anxious to get to work. When Ms. Harper gives the signal that it's time to go outside, they fairly fly out the door.

Destination: their flourishing garden plot in the community garden behind the church. The garden consists of two sections, together about an acre of rich Mississippi earth. Neat green rows cover their plot. Summer peas, cucumbers, squash, broccoli, string beans, and butter beans are replaced in winter by cabbages, turnips, rutabagas, leafy kale, collards, and mustard greens. All are planted and lovingly nurtured by Dorothy Jean Harper and her "Louisville lambs."

The group's avowed purpose is "to get our children and community involved in motivational activities," says Dorothy Jean. "The children get some exercise and they learn to work. They make some money, grow some food, and learn about cooking and the nutritional value that can come from the land."

Dorothy Jean has taken the children on field trips—to the Georgia-Pacific Plywood and Particleboard Plant and to the Rooted In Community conference in Little Rock. "If we're good, Ms. Harper is gonna take us to California next year!" says young participant Jaqual Johnson.

The kids set up a roadside stand and sell turnip greens at one dollar a bunch, sometimes raking in as much as three hundred dollars, which they reinvest in materials like seeds and fertilizer. The kids also take home food, which their parents and grandparents help them wash and cook.

"They need to know how to grow things," says Dorothy Jean. "Everybody needs to know how to grow things."

Located in northeastern Mississippi, Winston County's main attractions include the Choctaw Indian mound and the oldest continuously operated water mill in the U.S., which still grinds corn six days a week. Louisville is the county seat, with a population of seven thousand. The Chamber of Commerce building on Main Street dates from 1851, and the *Winston County Journal* celebrated its centennial more than a dozen years ago.

There are still some jobs in Louisville in the lumber industry, at a chemical plant, and at some factories that make bricks, industrial gloves, and other products. Dorothy Jean worked in quality control at a seat-belt factory until the owners moved it to Mexico. Though area population has been dropping, *Journal* publisher Joseph McCain stays optimistic.

"Newspapers all over the country are having trouble because young people get their news for free over the Internet," he says, "but we're blessed with an older population that keeps growing, so our subscriptions are up!"

The children aren't the only community gardeners participating. Louisville's former mayor owned a nursery and donated seeds, and Mr. Hudson, another avid gardener and retired school principal, contributes his time and more seeds as well. There is no farmers' market in the area, but the community is small enough that neighbors are happy to buy all the produce; word-of-mouth is all the advertising they need.

"That little spot," says Mr. Hudson, pointing at a square of greens, "will net us a hundred dollars tomorrow. My son makes three to four thousand dollars a year growing okra."

In the garden, four-year old Malaisia Savior pulls up a turnip green, and an older girl scolds her because it's too small. Mr. Hudson, ever the educator, sees an opportunity for a lesson.

"Listen here, children," he booms, his loud voice and knobby index finger a compelling attraction. "She didn't make a mistake—she pulled up that plant because everyone else was pullin' up plants. See, it's all a learning process. Let's give Malaisia a hand for having learned a lesson today!" Everyone claps. "Now Malaisia, learn to stand still."

The children continue pulling up plants, but after awhile they're brought together for another lesson.

"Y'all know what a fungus is?" asks Mr. Hudson.

All are planted and lovingly nurtured by Dorothy Jean Harper and her "Louisville lambs."

"Mushrooms!" yell the kids, in unison.

"Y'all know what this thing is?" he asks, pointing at an insect flitting its wings on a leaf.

"It's a cabbage looper," one answers.

"Going through metamorphosis," says another in rapid-fire succession.

Mr. Hudson continues, "What are the life stages of an insect?" Well prepared, the kids call out, "Eggs! Larva! Pupa! Adult!"

Mr. McCain has come to take a picture of the children for the paper. Everyone poses next to the 4-H garden spot sign in front of the vegetables.

"No hand signs, people," admonishes Dorothy Jean, "and you—pull your pants up!"

There is intermittent giggling and afterwards, the children all want to see themselves on the digital camera screen. It's snack time, and everyone sits down with little bags of organic pretzels stamped with the USDA logo. They're left over from the first annual youth agricultural and training conference that took place at Mount Moriah over the weekend. More than half the kids—and Dorothy Jean—are wearing the T-shirt. These kids don't need much convincing to eat the greens they've grown.

"I like my collards with hot sauce," says Daymon Crowder, "I'll drown them in hot sauce."

"I put hot sauce on my popcorn!" says Dylan Nicholson.

"I like cornbread with my mustards and collards," says Malexius Triplett.

Later, some of the parents and grandparents come by. The men carry in bundles of just-picked greens tied with twine. The women are discussing corn bread recipes.

"The parents here are so supportive," says Dorothy Jean. "All it takes is a phone call and they're here."

Since "retiring" from the seat-belt factory, Dorothy Jean has invested her prodigious energies into singing with the church choir and running the Winston County Self-Help Co-op. Her dedication has ramifications that extend beyond the borders of the church plot they tend. Along with instructing this group of kids on planting vegetables, she serves up some life lessons. "Show some respect!" is something they're used to hearing. Respect is a big message in East Mississippi, and Dorothy Jean wants the kids to learn respect for their parents, each other, and most of all, the church.

"All we're trying to do," she says, "is make them feel like everybody's somebody."

"I like my collards with hot sauce. I'll drown them in hot sauce."

Ancient Craft, Great Cheese

pennsylvania :
melanie & mark dietrich cochran

Melanie and Mark Dietrich Cochran make medieval cheese in a modern facility. Their family farm lies in a lush Pennsylvania valley near to where Melanie's great-great-grandparents worked the land.

Melanie and Mark bring a zest to their cheese by inventing original names for their various varieties. They also advocate taking lessons from earlier times such as the importance of raw milk, organic feed, and pasture-raised meat. Melanie quotes the owner of Restaurant Nora (the first organic restaurant in Washington, D.C.), "You can pay the farmer today or you can pay the doctor tomorrow." Melanie and Mark combine a love for old ways and traditions with progressive leadership towards sustainable local communities.

Mark and Melanie came from different worlds. Mark was a "Navy brat" from Virginia Beach who went to Virginia Tech to study English with an emphasis in medieval literature. He had worked in graphic design and never imagined becoming a cheese maker. Melanie, the daughter of two self-described hippies from the "back to the land movement," also attended Virginia Tech and studied dairy science. They shared a love for medieval reenactment that they still pursue today, stepping into the 1400s once a month at the Society for Creative Anachronism gatherings. Here all participants most obey two rules: you must dress from before the 1600s and you must be chivalrous and courteous to all.

Few cheese makers know the ancient beginnings and history of cheese making like Melanie and Mark. Their business is named "Keswick Creamery"—Keswick being an Old English name for a farm where cheese is made. "Cheese making likely predates recorded history," explains Melanie. "In Homer's Odyssey, Cyclops carried his milk around in an old goatskin and Odysseus found racks of cheese lining the giant's cave." Melanie goes on to say that Egyptian hieroglyphics dating to around 2000 B.C. show the cheese-making process, and the Romans created detailed cheese-making literature.

Mark and Melanie use natural calf rennet to make cheese from their milk, similar to how the Cyclops mythically made his cheese from goat rennet. Rennet is a substance that can be found in the fourth stomach of any ruminant and is a powerful coagulant that prevents the animal from over-eating by solidifying excess milk in the stomach. While medieval recipes called for adding a piece of a calf's stomach to milk, contemporary producers extract rennet from calves. Melanie smiles and explains that rennet is a hot button issue in vegan and farming circles, but that it's not actually an ingredient, but an enzyme that turns the milk into solid curds and liquid whey, and most of it drains off with the whey.

Mark and Melanie have about forty dairy cows which they milk twice a day and pasture on grass throughout the year, except in wintertime. Of the cows Melanie quips, "It's like being surrounded by thousand pound teenagers. They're quite rambunctious." Each cow has its own name and produces around forty to forty-five pounds of milk every day, of which half is sold to a local milk cooperative and the rest used for cheese making. Selling cheese adds value to their milk and also adds fun and family time as evidenced by how their young daughter Madelyn cavorts in her playpen near the production room as her parents labor over waxed wheels of cheese.

To refine their craft, Mark and Melanie have attended cheese-making workshops all over the East Coast, studying under respected European cheese masters. The workshops expand their technical expertise and inspire their creativity, resulting in new cheeses like "Dragon's Breath"—a pepperjack-styled cheese, and Wallaby—a monterey jack style named after one of their favorite cows.

Mark and Melanie make all of their hard cheeses with raw milk, and began this practice many years ago because of its cost-effectiveness. While much debate surrounds pasteurization, the Food and Drug Administration considers raw milk cheeses aged more than sixty days to be safe. Federal and state law require that fresh cheeses and yogurts be pasteurized (heated to kill bacteria), but beyond that the Dietrich Cochran's yogurt contains

"It's like being surrounded by thousand pound teenagers. They're quite rambunctious."

only their milk, a culture, and whatever type of organic fruit they add to each batch. Most mass produced yogurts add MPC (Milk Protein Concentrate) which is imported from countries like Ukraine and China as a "chemical" to avoid World Trade Organization tariffs regarding dairy imports. Unknown chemicals and additives like this make parents all the more excited about the all natural yogurt cups available from Keswick Creamery.

While most industrial dairy operations only milk their cows for two years, followed by an all-expense-paid voyage to the dog food factory, the Dietrich Cochrans, with their old-time philosophy of animal husbandry, obtain high quality milk from their animals for seven to nine years. Melanie's mom, Susan, and her husband have managed the herd genetics and registered their bloodlines. With her professional degree in dairy science combined with her organic and grass-feeding practices, Melanie has her feet in both worlds.

Keswick Creamery is a family farm if there ever was one. Melanie's sister, Emily, twenty-six, lives nearby with her boyfriend and teaches riding lessons on the farm to fifteen to twenty students with her thirteen horses. She plans to move to a nearby farm and begin a horse boarding business for up to twenty-five animals. Melanie's two younger brothers live on the property and work both on and off the farm. A young family friend, Clint, helps with milking and a variety of farm chores. While many farm workers in America don't get bonuses, Clint received his own cow for Christmas last year. Melanie laughs, "Clint is like a brother. He should be a brother."

The rolling hills and Amish communities of rural Pennsylvania create fantastic farming conditions, but for vibrant markets Melanie and Mark pack up their cheese, yogurt and ricotta and set up shop on Sundays at the Dupont Circle farmers' market in Washington, D.C. They also sell at markets in Tacoma Park, Maryland, and two others in the D.C. metro area, about a two-hour drive from their farm.

While Keswick Creamery has proven a hit with the metropolitan crowd, Mark and Melanie increasingly focus on building local sales. They are excited that several Pennsylvania restaurants now incorporate their cheeses into the menu and the couple sells their products at the local Carlisle Central Farmers' Market.

Mark and Melanie are active in their community. Melanie is on the board of the Pennsylvania Association of Sustainable Agriculture (PASA), has worked in the past as a 4-H leader, and has helped organize the district fair in years past. At PASA's 2006 conference, she led an all-day cheese track in collaboration with the Pennsylvania Cheese Alliance. She and friend, Sandy Miller, founded the Pennsylvania Farmstead and Artisan Cheese Association.

An educational and library space, a program for chefs to come learn about farming, hosting school farm visits, these are all on the list of ideas that Melanie and Mark discuss. Someday they hope to build an intern housing facility. Here they could host farm interns and instill their love and knowledge of cheese making to the next generation of this ancient craft's artisans. It's all about learning," says Melanie. "You can always learn more. You can be ninety years old and learn more."

Bucking the Trend

iowa : joel steege

Strolling into Steege's Meat Market outside Cedar Falls, Iowa will make your stomach growl. The rich, savory smell of fresh-cut, smoked bacon greets you to the tune of "She's Gone Country" drifting from a stereo in back.

In a nation where "mystery meat" and strange additives abound, Joel Steege specializes in slaughtering locally-grown livestock and preparing meat for the very families that raised the animals. Joel opened the business with his wife, Liz, and father, Larry, at the young age of twenty-four.

The Steeges base their business on quality and customer service. Despite steady growth, Joel, now twenty-nine, remains humble about his ambitions.

"I got into this business knowing that it's never gonna make me a millionaire, and that's fine by me. As long as I can pay my bills, support my family and come to work and enjoy it, I'm happy," he says.

Joel is the third generation in a line of butchers beginning with his grandfather, who ran a meat locker in rural Readlyn, Iowa, in the 1960s. Larry took over for his father in 1975, expanding the business to include

catering. Now the torch has been passed to Joel and Liz, who both work six days a week greeting customers and preparing meat cuts. Their first son was born early in 2005 and their second child in late 2006. With the right encouragement, the Steege family may soon watch its fourth generation of meat processors learn the secrets of the trade.

Steege's Meat Market lies amidst the long straightaways and looming silos that speckle the heart of Iowa corn country. Liz and Joel enjoy living in a small community because the people are trustworthy and have a laid-back attitude. What Cedar Falls may lack in big city attractions, it makes up for with small town charm and friendly neighbors.

Joel adds, "I've grown up in a rural area my whole life. You've gotta drive to get anything you want or need, but it's quiet and everybody knows everybody."

Joel went to nearby Hawkeye College to get a degree in horticulture, but decided that the world of plants and the monotony of Iowa landscaping jobs wasn't for him. He yearned to meet customers face-to-face throughout the day while responding to individual challenges.

Liz, twenty-seven, feels privileged to work with her family and friends, but acknowledges that it is difficult to balance work and home life. With two young children, Liz and Joel can hardly find a moment of free time.

The Steeges specialize in custom slaughter and processing for small farmers who bring in their own cattle and hogs. After the Steeges slaughter, skin, cut, and package the meat, customers return to pick up hundreds of pounds worth of ground beef, rib-eye steaks, bacon, and other cuts. Custom slaughtering accounts for about 80 percent of their business, while the rest comes from retail sales of processed meats.

Joel explains, "You bring your own animals in and you get your own meat back. That's a big thing people like. They like how they raise it and they like how it tastes." During hunting season, the market also custom processes wild game for customers— antelope, elk, deer.

Most of the farm animals the Steeges process are raised on pasture. Feedlot operations work with industrial-sized slaughterhouses, not family operations like the Steeges. As he slices bacon, Larry says, "People are tired of the boxed beef and the prepackaged meat from the grocery store."

Joel and Larry remain optimistic that demand for their services is growing and people are reawakening to the appeal of local foods and the unique taste of meat from small operations. Custom slaughter is not only better tasting, but provides livestock farmers with more affordable food, since they already own the meat and only pay for the slaughter and preparation.

The retail cooler brims with Italian sausage, cooked bratwurst with jalapeño peppers and cheese, smoked bacon, summer sausage, smoked pork link sausage, smoked cheddarwurst, ground beef, ribeye steak, turkey breast, chicken, boneless beef chuck

"As long as I can pay my bills, support my family, and come to work and enjoy it, I'm happy."

roast, Iowa ground horseradish sauce, "Country Bar-B-Q Sauce," and eight kinds of Wisconsin cheese.

"I try to familiarize myself with every customer and make them feel like I'd want to feel whenever I go into a place," Joel says.

To help foster community spirit, the Steeges sponsor an annual golf tournament in Readlyn. "It's just kind of our way of thanking our customers for being loyal," Joel explains.

The tournament began nine years ago and has now grown to 180 people, with a sizeable waiting list of people craving to chow down on the delicious food available at the Steeges' all-day open grill.

Larry began a catering operation that has blossomed with the addition of a large mobile smoker that hitches up to their truck. They cater large events on the weekends, serving up homemade brats and burgers as they socialize with the local community.

The Steeges have much to look forward to, with two young children and a steadily growing business. As more local residents choose quality local meat over industrial alternatives, and more farmers want to taste the meat they've personally raised, Steege's Meat Market will continue to grow as it fills an important niche in this agrarian community.

Native Wines, New Connections

nebraska : tim nissen

It's April, and the vineyard has survived a late freeze. On a windy Saturday, Tim Nissen, thirty-four, and his older brother Dave spend the morning planting new vines and trimming back existing ones to prepare them for Nebraska's summer growing season. They've hired a few neighborhood youth to help with trimming and pulling the old vines out of the way.

Tim takes pride in giving young people a productive way to earn a little cash and do some good, old-fashioned farm work. He likes working with local youth and often gets kids from the same families, younger siblings taking the place of their older brothers and sisters that have graduated high school and moved on. "It's really neat to see the kids grow year to year," he says, "it's one of the more rewarding parts of the business."

When you drive down Broadway Avenue in Hartington, a town of approximately 1,700 in the rolling hills of northeastern Nebraska, you pass by the Hotel Hartington, a turn-of-the-century brick building with covered windows and a faded, peeling sign. The bowling alley next door has been closed for a while, and the only buzzing business visible from the intersection of Broadway and State Street is Casey's gas station, a few blocks down the hill. The nearby town of Coleridge, Tim says, is just shy of being a ghost town.

Tim comments, "One reason rural Nebraska is depopulating—why the young people move away and never come back—is that they don't see a way to live in rural areas aside from what their parents or neighbors do. And if your parents don't seem very happy doing what they're doing, why on earth would you want to keep doing it?" He continues, "Until we recognize that mainstream contemporary agriculture is not always appealing to rural youth—or urban youth, for that matter—and until we do something about promoting alternative approaches to agriculture and other vocations in the rural U.S., we are going to see more towns going the way of Coleridge."

Tim is encouraged by the local poet and the local stained glass makers, but feels there is a long way to go in building awareness and understanding of the appeal of the countryside. This is what it will take to convince young people to settle in rural areas and embrace a rural way of life. Part of this appeal is found in unusual farms like the Nissens and others in his area. A dynamic group of forty-two farms in his small area are either organic or transitioning to organic, leading organic distributors to come here to source hard to find crops from the region. This growing network of organic farms is making small farming more viable and fighting the trend towards agricultural consolidation.

Tim grew up near Bow Valley, an unincorporated town just north of Hartington. His four-hundred-acre farm lies just one and a half miles from the land his great grandfather tilled in the 1880s. Tim's dad bought the farm in 1956, and farmed it just like his grandfather had done nearby. Deep roots mean that the Nissens have a lot of cousins and extended family in the area. A few years ago, Tim and his brother decided to use some of the family's pasture land to create a vineyard. They started planting grapes, wild plums, and chokecherries. Their vision? A fully functional, family-run vineyard supplied by a couple hillsides planted with sustainably grown fruits. These slopes, once vulnerable to erosion, now hold firm with deeply rooted vines and grass anchoring them down.

In 2007, Nissen Wines entered its fourth season, which meant some of the grape vines came into maturity. The twelve-acre vineyard includes four acres of wild plums, and one and a half acres of chokecherries. The family has already made wines from the these fruits. The wild plum is Tim's favorite. He explains, "It's a totally original taste that you simply can't find anywhere else." These indigenous fruits are relatively easy to grow, but challenging to turn into clear, marketable wines.

The first public wine tasting—after the fall 2007 harvest—was a memorable affair. Many wine tastings later, the Nissens are well on their way to establishing a loyal clientele and are attracting people from over thirty miles away. They now offer seven different wines, and thirteen stores in two states have already picked up and are selling their wines.

The business is young and growing, to be sure. Tim hopes that as appreciation for local, organic, and sustainably-grown products grows, so too will his market share. "Organic farming practices are not just environmentally important," he says, "they are a fundamental consumer issue. Farms should be responsive to customer demand and I'm trying to listen to the concerns of my customers."

Tim is looking forward to the return of farm visits. "The recent growth of agritourism is a sure sign of our cultural need to return to the land and reconnect with farmers," he says.

"One reason rural Nebraska is depopulating—why the young people move away and never come back—is that they don't see a way to live in rural areas aside from what their parents or neighbors do. And if your parents don't seem very happy doing what they're doing, why on earth would you want to keep doing it?"

While Tim and his brother both have off-farm jobs, they're working on a new business plan to see if jumping in full time makes sense. Dave and Tim enjoy working together and often find themselves on the same page. "It's kinda eerie how we think alike!" he exclaims.

Tim and Dave have benefited enormously from the mentorship of other vintners and grape growers in the area who have shown openness and eagerness to help younger growers get started. With the ease of Internet communications and the wealth of online resources available, Tim can be connected to others in his craft from all over the world. He also finds support more locally from the Nebraska Sustainable Agriculture Society and the University of Nebraska.

These enthusiastic vintner brothers are bachelors, and when asked about this Tim quips with a wry smile, "Yeah, that's one of the only drawbacks to living in a rural area." But with more visitors coming to the farm, who knows? As Tim remarks, "Everybody loves wine, all over the world."

With Love and Prayer

michigan : jesse & betsy meerman

The ingredients list on a package of Jesse Meerman's cheese lacks the usual gibberish that only the most learned of consumers would understand. It lists only simple, natural ingredients, such as milk—and it ends with "love," "bravado," or "prayer."

Jesse chuckles as he explains that the USDA inspector surprisingly didn't mind these intangible ingredients. Every family member at Grassfields Farm has a role to play and unique skills to bring to the table, no matter how young or old. Jesse and his wife, Betsy, hang some bumblebee decorations over the bed of their three year old daughter, Sophia, hoping that one day she may just become the family beekeeper. And with the recent birth of their second daughter, Katie, they feel confident that a fifth generation of Meermans will preside over these pastures.

Although Jesse is only thirty-one years old, the Meermans have been on this fertile land near Lake Michigan since Jesse's great-great-grandfather arrived in 1882. Their broad fields and woods lie in rural Coopersville, Michigan, where long straight roads lead past many active farms and agricultural businesses. The Meermans are devoted Christians, like many in their nearby community, and cheerfully perpetuate the Midwest's reputation for friendliness.

The agrarian tradition has been passed down through four Meerman generations, but not without times of great difficulty and crisis. The 1980s were an especially hard decade for family farms. Many went under due to rising input costs and stagnant commodity prices. The Meermans soon realized that they could not afford to

"We're not just responsible to the USDA, we're responsible to our customers."

continue their dairy operation in the "college style," where cows were kept contained, fed special feed mixes, and the whole system was highly mechanized. In 1991, Steve Meerman and his sons decided they had to try something new or quit altogether.

The family decided to go back to pasture grazing their animals, allowing them to graze on "God's natural bounty of fresh growing grass" instead of buying corn and hay. They slowly noticed improvements in production and animal health, and soon enough they were back on their feet as a family dairy. The Meermans were one of the first farms in the region to switch back to pasture grazing, and they now see a strong movement building among farmers to return to a more natural course. They were certified organic in June 2007, which translates into higher prices for their milk and produce and ensures customers of their long-term commitment to the health of their land and animals.

"It's really catching on now," says Jesse, referring to organic farming, "especially in the milk industry."

Jesse went off to college in 1997 for a year and a half, playing competitive soccer and studying a variety of disciplines. Then news came that his father had cancer. He then returned to the farm to live and work as his dad recovered. Sadly, Steve passed away in 2007. Now the youngest Meerman brother, Jay, has taken over his share of the work, keeping this family farm strong and honoring their beloved father.

The Meermans maintain a diverse mix of chickens, cattle, pigs, ducks, and goats (for cheese) along with large vegetable gardens—all of which end up on the Meermans' plates and those of the local community. Jesse knew that their most valuable resource was the rich and nutritious raw milk produced by their 140 dairy cows. He didn't like to see this resource degraded by the homogenization and pasteurization processes, which destroy all of the beneficial bacteria and much of the vitamins and calcium in milk. Pondering this dilemma led Jesse to try cheese making as a way to add value and take advantage of the health benefits of raw milk.

After much research and family discussion, the Meermans set up a cheese making facility next to their milk storage barn. They've gradually scaled-up production to two thousand pounds of cheese per month. Because of their Dutch ancestry, the family chose to craft Dutch cheeses like Leyden, Edam, and Gouda. It was this interest in their roots which put them on the path to making these rare Dutch cheeses.

To lock in fresh quality, Jesse makes cheese in the afternoon directly after the noon milking when the raw milk is just minutes old. During the summer, Jesse and his older brother, Luke, milk the cows at noon and at midnight. They follow this unusual schedule because the hot noon sun makes the cows uncomfortable. Bringing them in the barn at this time provides a better cycle for the animals and reduces their stress. In the colder months, Jesse and Luke revert to a more common 4 a.m. and 4 p.m. milking schedule.

As Jesse tours the farm, he bends down and runs his fingers through various kinds of grasses, rattling off their names, attributes, and the nutritional value for the animals. He resembles a scientist, excitedly explaining a new invention. The taste and quality of Jesse's cheese ultimately come from this grass, therefore, it is vital that he understands the soil and ecology of the farm. Being natural and organic just makes sense to the Meermans. They believe this is closer to the way God intended farming and are happy to distance themselves from today's synthetic chemicals and genetically modified organisms.

Raw milk, despite its potential health benefits, cannot be sold in Michigan because ensuring the uniformity and cleanliness of raw milk would require many regulations. Requiring milk to be pasteurized is a much simpler option. The Meermans legally drink their own raw milk, which has a uniquely rich and fresh taste. The Meermans maintain a very high level of sanitation and quality in order to drink their milk raw, whereas the dairy industry allows lower quality milk to be sold to customers simply because it has been pasteurized.

Jesse is one of very few Michigan farmers to pioneer "Herd Share," whereby local families can purchase one-tenth shares of a small cow herd. They then can come to the farm to pick up their share of the cow's raw milk from the Meerman's refrigerated containers. Jesse learned of the idea from another farmer in Eastern Michigan and has USDA approval for the venture.

Jesse attributes much of the demand for their natural produce to concerned mothers who want the most nutritious food for their children.

Jesse, Luke, and their wives, Betsy and Vicky, enjoy the Herd Share program because, although it's not highly profitable, it unites a like-minded community and brings a constant flow of visitors to Grassfields Farm. The Herd Share customers often stop to chat, passing along knowledge and building enduring friendships. These small interactions form the backbone of an ever-changing community and help the customers feel some ownership of the farm.

"We're not just responsible to the USDA, we're responsible to our customers," Jesse says. When customers pull into the shaded farm house area they can enter Grassfields farm store, a room packed with refrigerated cheese, chicken, eggs, bacon, ham, ground beef, steaks, and lamb. This entire mix of products comes from the Meerman farm. They also carry other Michigan products, from maple syrup to miniature farm equipment toys and T-shirts. In the back of the store lies a comfy, overstuffed chair where guests can rest and chat with whichever family member is attending the store at the time. Children's books and toys lie scattered around the chair, an entertaining diversion for the young ones while their parents pick up some produce or swap stories.

Visiting with customers and giving them tours of the farm not only ensures that the Meermans maintain a high standard of quality on the farm, but it also helps them educate consumers. The Meermans throw big open houses to commemorate special events complete with farm tours and demonstrations of various farm activities. Jesse invites school groups, fellow church members, and other farmers out to learn about the family business. The Meermans also helped establish a pasture grazing association where farmers open their farms and financial books to each other in order to share wisdom and keep family farms fiscally successful.

Jesse attributes much of the demand for their natural produce to concerned mothers who want the most nutritious food for their children. He laughs because his wife Betsy, a physician's assistant, often leans more towards traditional medicine, while he constantly wants to try natural remedies. He believes good health is linked to keeping the land and animals as natural as possible. To prove his point, he explains that when they switched the calves from the milk replacer advocated by university scientists to their own raw milk, they noticed a marked improvement in the calves energy and growth.

The Meermans want to remain a family farm long into the future and keep looking for creative ways to make it possible. By educating and interacting with the community, they hope to maintain a tight link with their customers. Jesse, wearing a goofy-looking soccer ball over his hairnet while he mixes the curds for his cheese, acknowledges that he owes everything to his family, his wife Betsy, and his faith, which has guided them to this place.

Sowing a Food Community

idaho : soil stewards

Stepping out of the ivy-covered Agricultural Sciences building at the University of Idaho on harvest day, there is a crispness in the afternoon air. Though it's early August in northern Idaho, freezing temperatures might only be a month away. But today the skies are clear and blue in every direction and there are six good hours of sunlight left to pick, dig, gather, and pull summer's bounty from the field.

The Soil Stewards is an organization founded in 2003 by a dedicated group of students. Its goal: to create and support a student-run organic vegetable farm in Moscow, Idaho. With a diverse membership that includes faculty, staff and community members, the organization gives a face to sustainable and organic agriculture efforts within a traditional land grant university system.

The group rents nearly three certified organic acres within the larger Parker Plant Science Research Farm—a 150 acre plot of University land where future staples of global agriculture are created. Most of these rolling Palouse fields are dedicated to conventional and no-till wheat research; foundation seed production for wheat and Idaho's famous potatoes; a breeding program for canola, mustard, and other edible and biofuel oilseeds; and a forest nursery growing native and adapted species for reforestation and urban landscapes.

But the southernmost edge of Parker Farm looks quite different from the surrounding quilt-like squares of traditional agronomic crops, and the Soil Stewards hope it will contribute to the future food system as well. Here, north to south running rows boast every shade of green, with varying textures and occasional bright spots of color. More than eighty varieties of vegetables, herbs, and cut flowers make up this lovely tapestry. Some rows are blanketed with a floating row cover, giving the odd impression of interspersed patches of new fallen snow. This is the Soil Stewards farm.

Ariel Agenbroad squeezes into her beat-up green Subaru dubbed "the truck," to make the two mile joureny to the farm. The truck is stuffed top to bottom with tools of the trade: a dozen heavy duty plastic vegetable crates, numerous hand tools, a digital scale, all manner of produce bags, twist ties, Korean harvest knives, and a red Earthway Seeder seatbelted in the passenger side. Often a volunteer or two pile in as well.

At any given time, twelve to twenty volunteer members grow, harvest, and sell fresh produce through a Community Supported Agriculture program (CSA), a weekly campus farm stand, sales to university foodservice, and occasionally, local retail outlets.

Volunteers can receive organic produce or academic credit in exchange for labor.

At the farm, Ariel spots Lydia Clayton, wearing a straw cowboy hat and flowered shirt, her sleeves rolled up. Known for the delicious carrots that are part of her research, Lydia has confessed to deeper feelings for another below-ground crop—the humble allium. "I think I want to be an onion farmer," she says.

Chris Chandler is also at the farm and as usual is not wearing shoes. Chris is a senior dietetics and nutrition major and an honored Barry M. Goldwater Scholar. He's been a member since his freshman year. His interest in farming stems from his commitment to hunger issues. His dream is to help communities in developing nations learn to feed themselves from the ground up, sustainably.

Heidi and her eight-year-old daughter, Emmaline, are already at the farm as well, the latter suddenly appearing from underneath the trellised cherry tomato vines. "I'm taste testing," she confesses. "'Sungold wins!'"

The sun is setting as the students bundle the last bunch of "Bright Lights" Swiss chard in the waning light. Looking around at the equally bright, accomplished student leaders who, minutes before, were giggling excitedly as they dug for potatoes on their hands and knees, Ariel wonders how these experiences will shape their perceptions, politics, and roles as active citizens of a sustainable future. She says, "The Soil Stewards farm project has reached out to students and community members from many backgrounds, connecting us all to the art and science of growing food for others and ourselves. We are learning to take our place within the larger food system, and anxious to share our discoveries." The ripple has begun, and the effects might just change our world.

Lydia has confessed to deeper feelings for another below-ground crop—the humble allium. "I think I want to be an onion farmer."

six : culture & community

The ties that bind communities come in countless forms—shared interests, places, arts, traditions, trades, and heritage are only a few—yet they all spark connections between people that make lives richer. Like all communities of place, rural towns depend on active citizens to thrive and grow stronger. And active citizenship must be embraced by the young if we are to have hope for a better world. The stories here suggest a bright future.

On the following pages, we hear about dancers, architects, artists, and musicians who are using their art to tell stories, give people opportunities, and connect to traditions. From a dance studio in a small Kentucky town to a Cajun music festival in Louisiana, these young people are taking strings from the past and weaving them into a promising future.

Glimpsing into the lives of community builders from all walks of life allows us to explore our own passions and talents and discover how they might be used to strengthen our own communities. In this chapter, we share the stories of youth making vital contributions to the places they call home, while at the same time turning their own dreams into reality.

En Pointe in Kentucky

Kentucky : lora jane benedict

At the age of seven, Lora Jane Benedict knew she wanted to be a dancer. That's when she got to take her first and only year of dance classes. That solitary year of classes was enough to inspire the artistic young girl to seek out dancing everywhere.

Still, there was another force in Lora's life that would weigh in on her future: her father—who worked as a miner and repairman in Eastern Kentucky's unpredictable coal mining industry. Rather than dance, he encouraged her to follow a path that would secure her financial future. Lora was torn.

"I just couldn't let it go," she remembers. "For Christmas one year, I begged my parents to buy me a year of dance classes. . . . Dad always said I was chasing after foolish dreams."

Far away from her family's home on the eastern edge of the state, she made a decision to follow the one dream that had always haunted her. For the first time since she was seven, Lora began taking dance classes, and finally, she found her calling.

Yet Lora didn't let the lack of opportunities to dance prevent her from keeping her body in peak physical condition. She swam competitively for seven years and stayed active in other school sports. Still, Lora reflects, "all the athletic comings and goings didn't fulfill that creative outlet for me."

When the time came for Lora to begin her academic career, once again she felt stuck between her own dreams and the hopes her family held for her. After dabbling at the local community college, and at Morehead State University, she enrolled at Western Kentucky University in Bowling Green. Far away from her family's home on the eastern edge of the state, she made a decision to follow the one dream that had always haunted her. For the first time since she was seven, Lora began taking dance classes, and finally, she found her calling.

When she began dancing as an adult, Lora had to make up for many lost years.

"It was very hard because I had to play catch up. All the other students at Western had danced all their lives, or most of their lives," she recalls.

But with hard work and dedication, Lora not only caught up, she excelled, choreographing her own pieces at the university, performing in the downtown Bowling Green Capitol Arts Building, and, ultimately, being offered a position as a dance instructor in Panama City, Florida. But instead of heading towards the beach upon graduation, Lora took her skills back home to Paintsville, Kentucky.

Lora taught at Pikeville College while she formulated her plan to open a dance studio of her own. In September of 2004, she christened Pointe of JOY in the Paintsville Recreation Center. It had concrete floors and no mirrors, except—Lora notes with a smile—once the sun went down, some of the windows functioned as makeshift mirrors. After moving to another location for a year and continuing to build her clientele, she acquired a business loan from the Mountain Association for Community Economic Development (MACED) and purchased a beautiful downtown Paintsville building, Pointe of JOY's permanent home.

MACED, a business development organization, serves fifty-one Appalachian counties in eastern Kentucky. It offers a variety of services to invigorate local economies and help low-income individuals achieve their goals, financial or otherwise. MACED conducts research, makes educational opportunities available, provides resources, and offers technical support and financial backing for small businesses to improve employment opportunities and economic stability. While MACED's initiatives go well beyond financial assistance for small businesses, for Lora, that was all she needed to hit the ground running.

Getting the MACED loan was no small matter, as Lora, still in her early twenties, was required to have a co-signer. Her parents agreed, but, she notes, "This was a very big deal." By signing on her loan, they were risking everything they had.

That was a lot of stress for the young businesswoman who wasn't even sure if she wanted to stay in Paintsville. But when Pointe of JOY staged its first local performance, it became clear to both Lora and her parents that they had made an important investment. That performance, in Paintsville's Ramada Inn, brought in an audience of two hundred people.

"Up until that point," Lora reflects, "my dad thought I was still chasing my dreams. But then he saw me dance." Lora recalls the audience's reaction when she went up *en pointe*. The whole place hushed. "Once I finished performing, I looked up and my dad had a dozen roses and was coming at me. Finally, my dad believed in me," she says emotionally.

Since then, business has been booming. In spring 2006, Lora offered more than twenty classes and had more than one hundred clients. Classes include ballet, jazz, ballroom dancing, yoga, Pilates, and acting—with options for different age groups and ability levels.

Beth Slone, a seventeen-year-old dancer in Lora's pointe class is thrilled by the opportunity for small class instruction at Pointe of JOY.

"I've learned so much coming to Lora. She's phenomenal. When I danced in Prestonsburg, with twenty to thirty girls in the class, I just danced. There wasn't the technical training," she says.

In Painstville, Beth is in a class of three, and receives the kind of personal attention she believes will allow her to pursue her own goals in dance. Like Lora, Beth would like to provide quality dance opportunities in rural areas, where they are needed most. Beth recently was accepted to the dance troupe at Eastern Kentucky University and at the conclusion of her first year was presented the "Most Outstanding New Dancer" award.

"The business really prides itself on giving students personal attention," Lora says. "That's the draw for most of our students." Classes at Point of JOY range from three students to around twenty, and they are distinguished by Lora's interest in incorporating theory-based textbook training.

"Even the four-year-olds take notes in class," she says of her teaching style. "I feel that you have to have the intellect to back up the talent."

Dedication to her dancers is indicative of Lora's overall business philosophy. Her mission is simple with Pointe of JOY: "I try to teach my students more than ballet; I try to teach them something about life and character. I think they eventually figure out that what I'm trying to do is help nurture upstanding community members."

Lora now commutes forty minutes to Inez, Kentucky, to teach more classes. A show there in June 2006 had more than ninety-two performers. Extending her classes to Inez has proved to be a savvy business move, boosting her total clientele by 50 percent. More importantly, it is another opportunity to bring dance to a community in need.

"Inez has little formal training available in dance. They can get the booty-shaking stuff from high school dance teams, but the real technique, they don't get," she says, laughing.

Lora was recently appointed to the Kentucky Arts Council Education Roster, enabling her to work in schools teaching dance during the day, while continuing her studio in the evenings and on weekends. Teachers work with Lora to apply for grants to introduce kids to dance—beyond the booty-shaking stuff.

Lora married "her dream man," Jason Benedict, in 2007. He shares many of Lora's values, and works as the president of a community non-profit called Good Neighbors Inc. Not surprisingly, they met after a parade at the Apple Fest where Lora's students were performing.

Despite all of the hard work and endless dedication, not to mention the pressure involved in starting up her own "hometown" business, Lora Jane Benedict has found her niche. Evidently, she knew this when she named her business. Pointe of JOY is a source of inspiration and elation for her dancers, her growing audience, and, she hopes, for the greater Paintsville community.

"I try to teach my students more than ballet: I try to teach them something about life and character. I think that they learn eventually that what I'm trying to do is help nurture upstanding community members."

Blackpot Festival & Cookoff

louisiana : glenn fields

Syncopated drumbeats, swinging fiddle melodies, and an accordion's asthmatic whine echo through a darkened parking lot. They're drifting up from a passel of eleven mud and hand-hewn cypress timber houses, a re-created Acadian village and the setting for the South Louisiana Blackpot Festival & Cookoff.

Stageside, the sound is loud enough to rumble anyone's insides. Most surprising are the youthful faces of the musicians onstage. Three intense twenty-somethings ardently tease notes out of f-holes, voice boxes, and amplifiers, sending the music up and down, cresting and crashing, for a crowd a few hundred strong. Some dance energetically, a whirl of skirts and denim; others sway peacefully; those on the picnic benches dig vehemently into po'boys and bowls of gumbo. Despite the late calendar date, it still feels like summer.

A group of disheveled-looking college students occupy one of the picnic blankets.

"We love the music, the heritage, the dancing, being outdoors," says Lacey Dupré-Bacqué, a master's student in organic gardening at Louisiana State University. "This corner of Louisiana is special because our traditions are rich, abundant, still very much alive, and maintained by young people."

Indeed, smatterings of French—both Parisian and Acadian—erupt at random. As one woman, handing out samples from a local health food store says, "It's at festivals where everyone intersects: the hippies, the old-timers, the families."

Jeremiah Ariaz, a young art professor who's just moved to Baton Rouge from Los Angeles, admits to being surprised by how deeply he's enjoyed Cajun music and festivals like Blackpot.

"The South has a very distinct culture that's absent in a lot of parts of the country," he says. "But people here embrace it. It makes for a lot of fun."

The Blackpot festival began in 2006, and Glenn Fields, thirty-two, is the force behind this event. The Louisiana native plays drums for the Red Stick Ramblers, a Cajun band that's headlining the weekend festival. Glenn is on the road two hundred days of the year and loves being home.

"We play so many festivals that we wanted to take our favorite elements of the ones we like—the camping, the cookoffs—and combine them," he says.

Glenn elicited support from a number of local businesses—guitar stores, a Cajun music label, the local paper—to help sponsor the event. Fields and fellow organizer, Jillian Johnson, called their musician friends and put together a lineup fifteen bands strong. Local bands like Feufollet, the Lost Bayou Ramblers, the Lafayette Rhythm Devils, and the Pine Leaf Boys were more than happy to participate.

"The time was right," Glenn says. "It seems Cajun music is hip again. The popularity of Cajun music and culture swings back and forth—there was an upswing in the 1960s and 1980s, and now the pendulum's swinging back up again."

The Blackpot Festival is an annual event, and welcomes visitors from across the country—young and old alike—to join the festivities. A writer for *Smithsonian* who attended the festival, later wrote, "Twenty-somethings with tattoos shared the floor with dancers in their seventies, all of them swinging and swooping and hollering. Cajun culture, it would seem, is alive and well, and ready for another century."

One vendor summed it all up: "Compared to the processed pop music we hear today, Cajun music's totally organic. It's homegrown stuff. Nutritious, you know? That's why it feels so satisfying."

Steel Mills to Circus Arts

ohio : cirque d'art theatre

Appalachian towns hard hit by the loss of mining and industrial jobs often struggle just to get by, and they usually don't support a thriving arts community, let alone launch successful circus and dance programs for hundreds of local youth.

Cirque d'Art Theatre is the brainchild of Ohio native and former professional circus performer and dancer Pegi Wilkes of Portsmouth. Pegi teaches people, young and old, how to perform lively and creative circus acts that they never imagined they could accomplish. Pegi's former students teach most of the classes, which even the lowest-income students can attend, thanks to diligent grant writing, community support, and the group's passion for their art.

Students learn not just acrobatics and circus arts, but also teamwork and dedication. They often go on to dance in college and some even go on to professional circus careers. Success learning circus routines on gym mats and hanging hoops translates surprisingly well to success in their relationships and jobs.

Portsmouth sits on the northern banks of the wide and murky Ohio River in the Appalachian foothills of Southern Ohio, right on the Kentucky border. For the past several decades, big steel mills, uranium enrichment, and railroad businesses have slowly left the area. Population peaked in 1907 at 50,000, compared to today's roughly 21,000. The decline of heavy industry and lack of good jobs make it very difficult for many residents to get by, let alone pay for extracurricular activities. More than half of the performers in Cirque d'Art Theatre are on scholarships to attend the classes.

The young performers explain there isn't much to do in Portsmouth, which lacks a YMCA or recreation department and has only two movie theaters and a small mall. With a large studio space, friendly atmosphere, and skilled instructors, Cirque d'Art has grown from 50 students in 2003 to over 250 today.

Pegi returned to Portsmouth after she retired from the Vero Beach Recreation Department in Florida, where she originated a similar program—Aerial Antics Circus. She soon began working as the performing arts curator at the local Southern Ohio Museum. People began asking her to teach a small dance class for children, so Pegi applied for and received a couple of grants. That was the beginning of Cirque d'Art.

Pegi sits surrounded by several of her students. She says, "I've learned that the love of the art is sharing it, not in doing it yourself."

Cirque d'Art began officially on September 11, 2001—a difficult time to focus on the performing arts if ever there was one. Nevertheless, Pegi rented the studio with her own money and began offering circus classes to local youth. Cirque d'Art has a sliding-pay scale that goes down as low as fifteen dollars per month. Some of her students cannot even afford the smallest fee, so she finds local sponsors to make up the difference so that anyone can dance.

Trisha Schmidt is Cirque d'Art's assistant director and is also a physical therapist who works at the local Vern Riffe School. There she incorporates dance, movement, and circus arts into her programs for youth in wheelchairs and with other physical disabilities. This kind of unorthodox therapy not only helps improve coordination and health, but also provides a fun alternative to the typical routines of physical therapy. Trish began working with Cirque d'Arts in 2003 when she was thirty-two and her young daughter went on a field trip with her kindergarten class to see the circus. Trish called Pegi the next day and has been hooked ever since.

Courtney Speck, seventeen, has become one of Cirque d'Art's most talented performers, beginning to dance when she was twelve. Courtney plays the gargoyle in Cirque d'Art's haunted Halloween show. She eerily climbs up and down a rope as the public gasps at other ghoulish gymnastic feats. The show consists of acrobatic skits that reinterpret fairy tales: instead of Rapunsel allowing the prince to climb her hair, she strangles him! Pegi laughs and says, "Yes, we have a dark side!" She goes on to explain, however, that while circus dance may seem just like a fun after-school activity to some, it also teaches skills that could save one's life.

"Everyone should know how to climb up or down a rope or quickly descend a ladder backwards," she explains. The state of Ohio no longer considers physical education a mandatory part of the curriculum, so grant-driven programs must often pick up the slack. As America's youth become increasingly obese and inactive, dance provides a social, creative, and noncompetitive way for young people to get exercise and shrug off the stiffness caused by hours in front of a computer or television. Cirque d'Art creates an engaging social atmosphere and breaks down racial barriers as evidenced by the diverse array of students.

Heather White, seventeen, recently began participating after being persuaded by a friend. She was incredibly shy before beginning to perform with Cirque d'Art. "Everybody encouraged me to try new stuff and they accepted me for who I am," she says. The atmosphere in the high-ceilinged studio is one of mutual encouragement.

As America's youth become increasingly obese and inactive, dance provides a social, creative, and noncompetitive way for young people to get exercise and shrug off the stiffness caused by hours in front of a computer or television.

Students expand their capabilities one baby step—or contortion—at a time. In addition to attracting students from a wide range of ages and socioeconomic backgrounds, Cirque d'Art has a healthy contingent of young men participating as well. This is something that many performing arts classes don't see, especially among teenagers.

Jon Chandler, twenty-one, was very skeptical when he first attended a circus dance class, but soon discovered the thrill and intense physical challenge of tumbling and aerials. Physically strong and experienced performers like Jon often do adagio, where one person supports another in the air. Adagio requires that both performers work together and perfect their balance and timing as one or the other climbs and twists into the air. In the shows, only the more experienced performers take on these moves while younger performers turn cartwheels and complete more simple routines.

Since Cirque d'Art's founding, Pegi has seen remarkable progress in many young people. These circus dancers from the small town of Portsmouth, Ohio, have gone on to college, when no such plans existed before. Some have even become professional dancers. Performing with Cirque d'Art demands intense teamwork, physical problem solving, and the kind of dedication that can help youth succeed at virtually any task. Christin White, twenty, sums it up, "It teaches you to try anything. You may not be able to do it, but you'll try anything in life. And no matter what somebody throws at you, at least you'll know how to approach it."

Creating for 100 Years

illinois : nathaniel & kerry brooks

In a world of increasingly shoddy plastic tools and toys, Nathaniel and Kerry Brooks create dwellings and artwork that last for generations. As an architectural designer, Nathaniel specializes in historic restoration and preservation, rejuvenating generations-old structures. Nathaniel fights to save historic buildings in small town Quincy, Illinois, and designs new structures based on local traditions. Kerry is an internationally-recognized artist who brings art appreciation, shows, and fairs to the Quincy area, while painting portraits that may become heirlooms.

A small town allows this young, creative couple to make significant contributions to the community, to enjoy peaceful work time, and to actually sit down on their front porch for lunch together—a difficult task in larger urban settings.

In the rosy evening, Nathaniel relaxes in a wicker rocking chair on the wide front porch of the century-old house the couple purchased. Gazing through the large old willow trees, whose tendril-like boughs gracefully brush visitors as they walk up to the entrance, his trained eye surveys the neighborhood.

"Just on this one street you learn so much about the development of architecture in the U.S.," he says. The Brooks bought their home from a family who had owned it for over a century.

In addition to historic preservation, Nathaniel promotes New Urbanism, a style of architecture and urban planning characterized by mixed-use, walkable communities where centralized downtowns lessen the necessity for driving. Residential spaces top first floor retail shops, and zoning allows people to live near their work, parks, public buildings, and the stores that sustain them. This paints a rosy picture, but Nathaniel laments the fact that successful New Urbanism developments often price out low- and some middle-income residents due to their popularity.

Nathaniel went to Judson University near Chicago and met Kerry though their mutual friend Nadine. (Nadine now manages the Busy Bistro, a local restaurant housed in a building Nathaniel renovated.) Kerry got her bachelor's degree in Russian at the University of Illinois in Chicago. She lived in Russia and the Ukraine where she studied art in the academies in St. Petersburg and Kiev. The two art lovers were married in 2001. Kerry worked as a portrait painter while Nathaniel finished his Master's degree in Architecture. Then it was Nathaniel's turn to work for the Studio for Civil Architecture in New York, while Kerry undertook post graduate work at the New York Academy of Art.

Nathaniel still works from Illinois for his New York employer on restoration and design projects that often have him traveling across the nation from the tiny Quincy airport. He recently finished work on a Dutch colonial style house in Connecticut, built in the 1780s, which had suffered several haphazard additions in the 1950s and 60s. He re-exposed the original fireplaces that had been walled over and used reclaimed wood to complement the house's original broad floor boards. The Connecticut owners loved Kerry's paintings and bought several to adorn their home.

Beyond their professional work, both Nathaniel and Kerry involve themselves in the Quincy community. Nathaniel sits on the board of the nearby Gardner Museum of Architecture and Design and is a member of the Quincy Preservation Commission that evaluates all demolition permits and oversees historic structure modifications. He also participates in the Historic Quincy Business District, a group of local business owners that plans programs to promote local commerce. Recently, they brought free Wi-Fi access to the downtown and riverfront.

Nathaniel shakes his head as he explains how he fought to preserve historic buildings along Quincy's riverfront, and then got hired to help design condos in their place by the very people that demolished the older buildings. Nathaniel laments the disconnect between past and present; between a sense of tradition and modern development needs. His college thesis, "The Architecture of Civic Presence," dealt with these very issues, exploring how the built environment helps create community spaces and promote civic engagement. He believes that buildings not only teach us about our past and our heritage, but also help shape the future and influence our moods, relationships, and lifestyles.

Life in Quincy draws more young professionals than ever, as evidenced by several of the couple's college friends moving in and starting new businesses. In his office, Nathaniel works with Nicole, an intern from Judson who recently completed her bachelor's in architecture. Nicole commutes to work from her family's farm in nearby Hamilton, where she is the fifth generation to have lived on that land. At a time when small town America watches its youth leave for lack of jobs, Quincy, with its wireless access, riverfront, and restorations, seems to be experiencing a revival.

Half-squeezed paint tubes and intriguing portraits of women and landscapes fill Kerry's upstairs corner studio in their home. She recently created an installation at the local

hospital and travels to schools teaching students about art and being an artist. She finds it easier to get involved in small communities where most people often know each other. One of Kerry's recent projects has been a series of thirteen paintings of female friends and family members who have impacted her life.

"I'm kind of fascinated by the beauty I find in my friends and family. They're ordinary women, but each has their own personality and style," she says.

Both Nathaniel and Kerry create works of art meant to last, and both spend enormous amounts of time planning and designing their artistic endeavors. Nathaniel explains that most modern "stick-built," vinyl-sided houses often only last through the initial thirty-year mortgage before beginning to lose value, whereas well-built houses gain value over time and last for centuries.

He adds, "To me the task of architecture is wrought with responsibility because you're doing something that's going to last for hundreds of years."

Similarly, Kerry's portraits and other paintings become treasured family heirlooms that people use to connect with and remember their relatives.

The couple feels lucky to have been exposed to those in less fortunate circumstances and has decided to adopt a child or children from Kazakhstan. Kerry will teach their children Russian and help them begin an intercultural life without forsaking their heritage. Nathaniel and Kerry are eager to bring some more life into their antique house in Quincy and feel confident about raising children in the community. With their roots growing apace with Quincy itself, the Brooks' eagerly anticipate tiny new artists to join them.

"To me the task of architecture is wrought with responsibility because you're doing something that's going to last for hundreds of years."

The New Old Timer

"I grew up listening to my great-grandpa fiddle," says Todd Meade, with a gentle, dimpled drawl. "He lived to be a 101, but died when I was 7. I started playing after that."

Part-time university student and part-time, world-traveling fiddle player, Todd grew up on an eighty-acre farm that raised cows and tobacco. "Tobacco's not so good anymore," he says. "People are finding different things to farm." Thankfully, Tennessee has a growing industry that is much less pernicious to the lungs—music, and the tourism it attracts.

As a boy, Todd began weekly fiddle lessons with teacher Scott Gould. A quick study, he knew nearly 200 songs after five years. Soon he was jamming Tuesday nights in Bristol (the alleged birthplace of country music), Friday nights in Bluntville, and Saturday nights at the Carter Family fold in Hilton.

"Back when I was growing up, it was just me and a bunch of old men," he reminisces. "Now, there's a lot more interest in roots music."

In high school, Todd was asked to put a band together to fund raise for the National Honor Society. ("I wasn't in the honor society," he specifies, grinning.) Made up of classmates and relatives, the band, "Twin Springs," was such a success that they recorded a CD. It wasn't long before Ralph Stanley came knocking. Stanley gained widespread fame for his appearance in the 2000 movie hit, *O Brother, Where Art Thou?*

In the early 1950s, Ralph and his brother Carter Stanley were pioneers of modern bluegrass music, along with Bill and Charlie Monroe, Earl Scruggs, Lester Flatt, and a host of others. A Library of Congress Living Legend, Dr. Stanley has been called the best banjo picker in bluegrass. Now in his seventies, he still tours 200 days a year. Shortly after Todd's 18th birthday, Ralph handed Todd twelve CDs and said, "Learn these."

"The first time I played with Mr. Stanley was in front of a thousand people and a bunch of cameras," Todd recalls. "I was so nervous. He's such a legend."

On the job just a week, Todd was told, "'Pack your bags, tomorrow we're going to California for two weeks.' It was my first time ever on an airplane," he adds.

Todd spent 250 days on the road that year.

"I've been to every state in the continental U.S.," he says. "If I haven't played there, I've driven through it." He adds, wistfully, "We didn't do much other than play, though. I didn't see states so much as interstates."

After a year of touring, Todd enrolled at East Tennessee State University, the only four-year college with a bluegrass major. Half the week he tours with the band, Carolina Road. He plays bass and fiddle. Classes are squeezed into strictly delineated slots during the other half of the week, arranged so they won't interfere.

Critics deride bluegrass—a "modern" offshoot of old-time music—as "too Nashville"—in other words, too commercialized, too formal, too given to arrangement. Old-time music, Todd explains, is freer, looser. It's mountain music, whose melodies are sometimes recognizably Celtic. There are no solos, and often no lyrics; the musicians all play all the time, shuffling their bows or strumming their banjos "claw-hammer style." It's music that puts people in a dancing mood. They "flat-foot" or square-dance

"Back when I was growing up, it was just me and a bunch of old men. Now, there's a lot more interest in roots music."

or clog. The sound is highly local, and Todd claims he can tell the Carolina and Tennessee fiddlers apart.

"I like both," he shrugs. "My favorite, really, is old-time, but I can't make a living playing just that. And I love bluegrass too."

Undeniably, bluegrass has changed the face of roots music. *O Brother's* critically acclaimed soundtrack sold five million copies and propelled bluegrass and its melodic kin into the limelight.

"It proved we weren't just a bunch of bib-wearing, toothless hicks singing through our noses," says Todd. "Although some of the old-timers grumbled, it has made festivals a lot more hip and fun," he adds. Some of Todd's favorites are the Old Fiddler's Convention in Galax, Virginia, and the Appalachian Music Festival in Clifftop, West Virginia. Festival goers—and some performers—come from as far away as Europe, Australia, even Japan, and young and old alike jam until the early hours.

Savvy business leaders and politicians are adding roots and bluegrass music into their economic and cultural development plans—promoting local museums, instrument makers, and festivals. The music is ubiquitous, and formal jams are organized while informal ones coalesce at random. *Blue Ridge Country* magazine, with whom Todd collaborates, also works to promote tourism in the entire area. Nashville has its own branding agency, which markets and sells Music City as a "premier entertainment destination for travelers who seek authentic and unique leisure and convention experiences."

The bureau has fifty employees whose goal is to grow Nashville's second largest industry, which already garners the city three billion dollars a year. Although Nashville also houses the Museum of Tobacco Art and History, more people are coming to Tennessee for the music.

"It's a positive thing," Todd believes. "It can bring money into the area. People think they need factories, ATV trails, more logging—that it's okay for the mountain to slide into the streams." His voice falls to a whisper, takes on the tinge of the confessional: "I think I've become a bit of a Democrat!"

He blames the traveling.

Back at his apartment, Todd has a rehearsal scheduled with roommate and banjo-playing bandmate Josh Goforth. Besides the banjo and two fiddles, a mandolin is propped up against the wall and an upright bass case sits on the floor. When these two "college boys" begin practicing, exchanging wordless nods and looks, the melodies and harmonies of old-time favorites like "Arkansas Traveler" and "Angeline the Baker" seem to waft up through the rafters of their townhouse and float over the Wal-Mart and barbecue joints before fading into the cold Tennessee night air.

"It proved we weren't just a bunch of bib-wearing, toothless hicks singing through our noses."

Tribal Grounds & LIFT Culture House

north carolina :
leon grodski & natalie smith

"Some days we have knitting at five, art at seven, and heavy metal at nine, and some people are staying for all three," Leon Grodski says with a laugh as he describes the eclectic program offerings at LIFT Culture House in Cherokee, North Carolina. Leon and his partner, Natalie Smith, opened LIFT in 2004.

While Leon and Natalie were both at Western Carolina University, where Leon was an artist in residency, they crossed paths only a moment before Leon was to go to Europe. Like in the movies, they knew they wanted to be together, so they spent the next few months touring Slovenia, Italy, and Tunisia. Both wanted to come back and develop their concept of a "culture house," where people could come together to build a more vibrant community. Natalie had lived six years on the Cherokee reservation and knew the opportunity was waiting.

When they set out to open the coffee shop/cultural house, their goal was to create a place in their tourist-heavy community that not only served their original brand of fair trade coffee, Tribal Grounds, and deli-style vegetarian fare, but also hosted renowned local, national, and international art and cultural exhibitions. Within their first two years they had three exhibits in their art space, and an additional six in their communal areas. The first, "FLIGHT," received international attention, as it featured art work by Yoko Ono—singer, artist, and widow of John Lennon.

The main dining and performance area of LIFT is in the back, where a small art and Cherokee reference library are found in one corner and a red stage in the other. Booths made from reclaimed school bus seats line a wall, which also displays an art installation. Customers sitting under the exhibit bite into hearty breads and surf the Internet.

The overall effect of the art, décor, and food at LIFT, not to mention the grinding of coffee, contagious laughter of nearby patrons, and the couple themselves, is one of comfort and welcome. It is where people relax, talk, and celebrate weddings, anniversaries, and birthdays. There is even a free-speech night where the community gathers to recite poetry and talk about current issues.

Opening and maintaining the business has been no small feat. Natalie and Leon got their business development expertise from personal experience rather than from any formal business training. They would like to see additional support mechanisms locally for small businesses like theirs. Natalie points out there are things they just haven't had time to learn and she is sure other entrepreneurs face the same challenges.

For both community members and tourists to the area, LIFT represents one of the few Native-owned small businesses thriving in Cherokee. But Natalie and Leon are serving as inspiration for other tribal members and they believe there are many opportunities for more Native-owned businesses succeed.

Their goal was to create a place . . . that not only served their original brand of fair trade coffee, . . . but also hosted renowned local, national, and international art and cultural exhibitions.

Newbern Gets New Firehouse

alabama : Matt Finley

Matt Finley enjoys a hero's welcome when he visits the small town of Newbern. Back in college, while other students were buried in books, taking exams, and attending parties, Matt was living in this rural Alabama town, so small that you might miss it if you blink. As students in Auburn University's Rural Art Studio program, Matt and three classmates went to Newbern with intentions of creating something of lasting value for the community.

Newbern is quite a different world from where Matt now makes his home in Birmingham, just an hour and a half north. Just a little over a square mile in size, the town sits in the heart of Hale County in southwest Alabama. It's one of the poorest areas of the overwhelmingly impoverished Black Belt, so named for the rich, dark soil that once made cotton king in this part of the Deep South.

The flat stretch of state highway that serves as the town's main street sports only a few buildings. There's a mercantile store with old, dark pine floorboards that sells off-brand potato chips and hardware. Horns honk every few minutes as drivers greet neighbors walking across the store's gravel parking lot to the tiny post office next door.

Across the street is the town's first major building to be constructed in more than a century: the modern firehouse and town hall that was Matt's labor of love for two years. The slanted-roof structure is composed mainly of cedar, steel, and plastic-like polymer, but somewhat surprisingly, doesn't look out of place.

"Towns like this could go away," Matt says, as he drinks a glass-bottled RC Cola at Newbern Mercantile on a stifling May morning that already feels like the dead of July. "They just need new life and energy in order to not just fade away. All of these places are worth saving—they're worth devoting time and energy and attention to."

It was in front of the store that dozens of Newbern residents sat and cheered as Matt and his classmates erected the columns that support the building. That kind of support, from this small community of 231 people, kept the students going. "To see that much civic pride in a town that didn't have much to rally behind was pretty awesome," Matt says.

The Rural Art Studio is part of Auburn University's College of Architecture, Design and Construction. Matt's late professor, Samuel Mockbee, founded the program in 1992, based on his concept of "architecture of decency." The students use inexpensive, easily available materials to build high-quality homes and buildings for disadvantaged communities. "I was a floundering college student who had switched majors several times when I heard Mockbee give a lecture about the program," he says.

Matt's project began after the town received grant money for a new fire engine. To get the money, Newbern needed somewhere to keep the new truck. The prefabricated shed that had served as headquarters for the volunteer fire department wouldn't cut it.

Matt and his classmates spent six months creating the design for the building, which involved countless hours of consulting with professors, visiting architects, and the firefighters who would use the building. After the compromising of egos and creative differences, the four managed to agree on a barn-shaped, but contemporary style for the building, which would also serve as a town hall meeting space. But that was just the beginning. Forced to learn many skills as they went along, Matt and his friends became quick studies in welding, carpentry, and fundraising. More than 80 percent of the construction materials, totaling more than $100,000, were donated. With the exception of hanging the huge overhead garage doors, the students completed every bit of the work themselves.

There was no shortage of volunteers. The students sometimes turned away the townspeople eager to help out during the long, sometimes twelve-hour workdays. Even working all day, seven days a week, it took longer to finish the building than anticipated. Matt stayed on after he graduated to see the building through to completion.

Matt and his friends didn't just come into the town, do their thing, and leave. They immersed themselves in the community, even joining the volunteer fire department. They spent many nights enjoying home-cooked meals at the postmistress's home. They ran up a tab at the general store—a tab the owner never intends to collect.

Since graduation, Matt moved to Birmingham to start his career as an architect with Will Brothers, a business founded by one of his Rural Art Studio colleagues. But Matt plans to continue his work in rural areas. "Doing work in areas like these is rewarding because of the extreme gratitude people show," Matt says. "It wasn't until I moved away from Newbern that I realized how unique and special it was. People were immediately accepting, offering hospitality and generosity without reservation and without expecting anything in return."

"That kind of support from this small community of 231 people kept the students going. To see that much civic pride in a town that didn't have much to rally behind was pretty awesome."

environmental issues affect Alaskans. He knew what it meant to live in a community faced with erosion, change in weather patterns, and change in the migration of local animals.

Completely youth driven, AYEA works to inspire youth to take action on issues which they deem important. Started by six young people in 1998, today AYEA exists as a program of the National Wildlife Federation and functions as the statewide venue for youth education on civic engagement and environmental action. The program has provided leadership training to over a thousand youth, adult mentors, and peer leaders.

For Joe, the peer-to-peer philosophy of AYEA struck a chord because he loves to work with people. "I am an introvert, but when I work with people, I figure out more about my own passion for things. With AYEA, I don't have to hold myself back because I know I am working on important issues," he says.

AYEA has helped Joe see how he can make a difference. Prior to his involvement, he hadn't realized how his community's values towards natural resources were connected to the larger problems facing the environment. "Kotlik is kind of isolated from environmental news and opinions," he says. When Joe learned about the depth of environmental issues that face Alaskans, he realized that the connection between his village and the world was stronger than he had once thought. Now it is impossible for him to ignore environmental issues. "My generation will suffer the consequences of not acting now," he says.

Alaska is experiencing climate change in a way that the majority of the U.S. hasn't. The warming climate has caused more storms, resulting in erosion of the shoreline. Many of the villages, like Kotlik, are situated close to the shore for easier access to marine mammal hunting and fishing. In Kotlik, there has been extensive erosion of the beach where the village lies. Joe's own family saw a two-and-a-half-foot loss of land from one summer alone. For the past seven years, unseasonably warm weather has caused villagers to change their fishing and hunting habits. The difficulty is that climate change is not simply caused by the people living in Kotlik, or even in Alaska. The global nature of climate change means that the behavior of people around the world is impacting communities in the Arctic latitudes.

As part of "The Global Warming Campaign," Joe and other youth reached out to their peers across the state to teach them about the impacts of global warming on Alaska. The campaign collected signatures from more than 5000 high school students from 130 communities. The project went on to win the President's Environmental Youth Award in the spring of 2007. The result of the campaign was felt across the state, but was especially important for Joe and his peers at AYEA, who through the campaign saw the power of education and activism.

When you ask Joe about it, he is very down-to-earth: "It's not recognition or large-scale actions that make my work worthwhile, rather it is the small changes that I see in the people I work with that keeps me going. If someone walks away thinking about their actions more than they did before, it means it has had an impact." Joe adds, "You can't force someone to do something, but you can try to sway them just a little bit, and that is when I feel better about what I have done."

"My generation will suffer the consequences of not acting now."

New New Jersey

new jersey : mikey azzara

Speaking to a crowd of die-hard music lovers including the likes of Dave Matthews, Neil Young, and Willy Nelson, "Mr. Mikey" received wild applause—not for any musical showmanship—but for his overwhelming passion and dedication to local food, education, and community rejuvenation.

Mikey Azzara exudes an all-embracing, Italian-American enthusiasm and quasi-romantic love for fresh food, combined with a strong New Jersey accent and the fast-paced style of East Coast urbanites. Whether in his job coordinating outreach for the New Jersey office of the Northeast Organic Farming Association (NOFA), or as the founder of local farmers' markets and school gardens, Mikey focuses on community networking and tackling big tasks from as many angles as possible. Mr. Mikey, as flocks of local elementary school students call their twenty-seven year old gardening instructor, launches himself like a flushed free-range turkey into organizing local, state, and regional initiatives. He aspires to transform the very way that families eat.

When he entered Vermont's prestigious Middlebury College, Mikey had no idea what he wanted to do. He harbored no ambition to become an environmentalist or food activist, but Middlebury opened his mind. He got interested in organic farming. Soon his life's work would take him to his ancestors´ home of Italy as an organic farm volunteer, then back to his hometown of Lawrenceville, New Jersey.

Mikey was captivated by the joys of hard work on the land, cooking delicious healthy food, and biking through the Italian countryside. Amongst the agrarian splendor, though, he began to sense that Italy was not his home. It dawned on him that his home was not among the academic of Vermont either, but could only be found back in semi-suburban Lawrenceville, where he had all the connections to make a profound difference.

Mikey returned from Italy full of enthusiasm and inspired to dig his hands down into the dark American earth—planting the seeds for the next, more wholesome generation stateside. He applied for a job with the newly initiated Cherry Grove Farm and began work the next day.

"Seeing agriculture firsthand in the place where I grew up just blew my mind," he says. "It was like I was living in a different place."

Mikey became the farm's unofficial marketing manager, and Cherry Grove soon appeared in local newspapers nearly a dozen times. The editor of the *Trenton Times* bought a bag of salad greens, and two weeks later "Organic Farming Takes Root" graced the paper's front-page title.

Mikey brainstormed with Cherry Grove's owner, Matt Conver, about starting a farmers' market in Lawrenceville. The barber, Joe Guido, encouraged the two young entrepreneurs to hold it on Mondays, the day his shop is closed. Mikey stresses the importance of building relationships within the community. He has made agreements with everyone from the parents of childhood friends to his former baseball coach. His former coach, Carlos Hendrix, now runs the Lawrenceville Neighborhood Community Services Center. As the two strolled around the center grounds, Mikey pointed out that there was plenty of space for a garden.

No sooner had they put the first plants in the ground, than they decided to start a summer camp program, focused on gardening, cooking, and eating. As children plant carrots and summer squash, they also learn basic plant science from Mr. Mikey—like no book can teach. The camp's garden began as a simple ten-by-twenty-foot plot, then grew to fifteen-by-fifty. Today, the garden covers one fifth of an acre.

Mikey and his old middle-school principal started talking about how to bring hands-on food, biology, and nutrition education into the school's curriculum and cafeteria. Shortly thereafter, Mikey was meeting with high school administrators as well. They applied for a grant to have an all-organic day in the cafeteria and for Mikey to teach organic cooking to the junior class. Mikey´s Italian heritage, and the fact that his brother is a professional chef, adds authenticity and zest to his lessons.

Instead of confronting administrators and cafeterias to demand more organic food, Mikey strives to cultivate demand from the students. He started a food club at the

Mikey and his old middle-school principal started talking about how to bring hands-on food, biology, and nutrition education into the school's curriculum and cafeteria.

high school, and helped them install raised-bed gardens, an apple tree, and picnic tables on school grounds. Mikey asked teachers to make announcements to classes about the new club, and he was soon chaperoning students on farm visits, teaching them how to make ice cream, and screening films like *Fast Food Nation*. Students now run the club, which aims to get more local, farm-raised food into the cafeteria.

Last year, Mikey organized an open house for educators and administrators to learn about what was brewing in Lawrenceville. The superintendent of the district pressed Mikey, "How can we make this happen at all the schools in the district?"

Shortly after he began the public school outreach efforts, Mikey learned that NOFA New Jersey was searching for an outreach coordinator. He was torn between applying for a job that would enable him to make regional impacts and the thought of abandoning his budding efforts in Lawrenceville public schools. When NOFA agreed to help Mikey continue the programs while tackling regional coordination, he knew he had found the right job. Mikey organizes NOFA's large winter conference and their summer education conference, each drawing hundreds of farmers and organizers from all over the state.

Recognizing the importance of bringing together potential allies, Mikey organized a farmer-chef conference with seven chefs and seven farmers. Together, they made lists of products one demanded and the other supplied, and began directly sourcing local food to local eateries. The next conference ballooned to 150 chefs and farmers. Soon the Lawrenceville Culinary Partnership was born and the first "Taste of Lawrenceville" festival took off in October of 2006.

With programs, projects, and plans sprouting from all sides, Mikey attended the global Slow Food conference in Italy, in 2006, to share his story, and learn about organic food efforts worldwide. He was also one of four young farming advocates chosen to play a part in the 2006 Farm Aid concert. Prior to the concert, he participated in farm tours and sat on a panel with music legends Willy Nelson, Neil Young, and Dave Matthews. Before representatives from the national media, he talked about his efforts and explained their importance.

While feverishly organizing and networking to promote local food have afforded Mikey his share of time in the spotlight, nothing could strip him of his roots. Mr. Mikey's thick accent clearly shows that, despite widespread praise, an exceptional education, and international experience, he will always remain a hometown boy from Lawrenceville.

Standing Up for Change

new mexico :
colonias development council

Las Cruces is a friendly, if fast-growing, 70,000-person town at the southern border of New Mexico, cradled between the mountains and the mesas. If perhaps it lacks the romantic air of Taos or the turquoise tint of Santa Fe, it does boast psychedelic sunsets smeared across an infinite sky and a terrific burrito bar, the family-run Chihuahua's, where the flour tortillas are doughy and light to the point of being ethereal. Most of its unassuming citizens (university-affiliated, army, or retirees) would never guess that only a few miles south—and east, and also north—teem over thirty colonias, rural subdivisions inhabited by landowners, up to 18,000 in one community, who might lack potable water, wastewater systems, passable roads, or safe housing.

The Colonias Development Council (CDC) has known this for a while. The group has gone through as many names as it has self-conscious incarnations: beginning as the Farmworker Organizing Project (operating by means of the Catholic Social Ministries), morphing into the Colonias Organizing Project (a more radical social activist group), and finally, twenty years later, identifying as the CDC, a now solid, methodical group, most of whose nineteen members are younger than thirty.

If the CDC has transformed over the years, the problems they attack remain much the same. Mexican farmworkers—some documented, some not—have been living on small colonia lots, in some cases for decades. Eighty percent of them fully or partially own the land on which they live, as compared with the 64 percent state average. But the parcels of land they purchase from developers, who subdivide a sixteen-acre square into increasingly tiny bits, often lack basic amenities, easy access, and septic tanks.

The real estate contract fees are exorbitant and predatory, since residents often lack a bank account or credit history and make too little money to apply for loans. Those who miss even one payment are at risk of having their property seized, nullifying years of disbursement. The developers, for their part, claim that predatory practices, like a 15 percent interest rate, simply "minimize risk."

Rhetoric has it that the border patrol and the sheriff don't work together, but collusion is frequent; often, entire communities are locked down and searched with dogs. "At CDC, we've totally reconceptualized citizenship and are unconcerned about whether the homeowners are legal residents," says Megan Sneddan, who has been with CDC for seven years. Megan points out that many, having been granted amnesty in the 1980s or been landowners for ages, are legal. "Talk of illegality makes people suspicious, keeps them from coming to meetings, and in effect creates an anti-community," she says. We believe that if you're civically engaged, in other words engaged economically, politically, and socially, then you're providing a service to your society, whether or not you have the paper."

The cultivation of southern New Mexico's four main agricultural products—pecans, onions, chili, and cotton—has become increasingly mechanized, sloughing away available human jobs. Many citizens of the colonias have no experience performing tasks like opening a bank account, figuring out their taxes, or buying land. Often, families of four must make do on a yearly income of $12,000. Unlike many of the 1400 colonias in the state of Texas, New Mexican colonias usually have access to water, and increasingly to wastewater systems. Their biggest problem, instead, is substandard housing. Dodgy wiring often sparks trailer fires, and trailers built pre-1976 are ineligible for insurance.

Currently, CDC works with nine of the thirty-seven colonias in three neighboring counties. Mauricio de Segovia works with youth in two of them, preaching the gospel of critical thinking. "I want them to be civically engaged," he says. "I want them to question." As they complete their bachelor's degrees in accounting, Elva Varela and Erika Contreras teach finance on the colonias, both one-on-one and at night classes for parents at the elementary school. Lessons include how to file taxes, read a credit report, and choose a bank, for instance.

Patrick Wenger, a former intern, has taken on the issue of affordable housing by investing in a machine that produces cheap-but-sturdy compressed earth blocks from dirt, water, and a bit of cement. The idea is to build earth-block duplexes and greenhouses where people can grow vegetables to sell at the future farmers' market in Anthony—linking affordable, energy-efficient housing with economic development and food security. "This area is all agribusiness, so the only thing most people grow on their own are maybe green chilies," Patrick says. "They buy everything else at Wal-Mart or Sam's Club, depending on where the sales are." Building the earth-block homes would use local materials, local labor, and because adobe stabilizes temperature much more efficiently than thin trailer walls, energy costs would plummet.

A waste services conglomerate proposed building a landfill atop the colonia in Chaparral. With the help of CDC, community leaders took the case all the way to the Supreme Court. Members of another colonia, this one hundreds of years old, had spent two years planting a community garden, involving local children every Saturday morning and offering organic food courses. After the recent flooding, FEMA reclaimed the land for emergency housing, and the county granted their request. Twenty-two local families worked to fight the ruling, however, and the garden—so far—has been left untouched.

Megan has been working with a group of women to erect a child care center. Currently, the Columbus Center, a double-wide trailer, has twenty-four children and work for five part-time employees, but use of the facility fluctuates with peaks and troughs in the picking season. It could accommodate more children, but the seven-dollar-per-child daily fee exceeds what many can afford. "It's tough to manage, and far from sustainable," Megan says. "Most of the women stopped their education after second grade, so small-business skills are lacking, but how do you solve that?"

A long-planned day care center in Chaparral has expanded to include a commercial kitchen, sewing room, and multi-purpose room, but the original idea to build it from straw bales proved too expensive and the group has resigned itself to purchasing a quadruple-wide trailer instead. "Instead of something environmentally efficient that benefits local construction, we'll have to get a pre-fab building from out-of-state," says Megan ruefully. "Long-term, it's the worse investment, but it's all we have the money for. If we try to raise more funding, we'll lose the money that's already been granted, so we're kind of stuck." She sighs, "I wanted it as much as they did." Megan's at once disappointing and stimulating anecdote underscores the complexity of the organizers' work.

Ray Padilla, now a teacher at a local charter high school, managed a CDC youth center project in the 1990s that imploded after student artists graffitied a Zapata quote they considered inspirational on a mural. Some locals interpreted it as incendiary and ordered it removed. Although Legal Aid lawyers rubbed their hands gleefully at the prospect of an easy court victory, too few of the parents were willing to represent their children in the case. Many of them worked at the school cafeteria or as teacher's aides, and they had too much to lose.

"It was a lesson in power relations," says Ray. CDC now approaches its work more moderately, less "in-your-face," as Megan calls it. "We have to balance economic sustainability while at the same time keeping on with the organizing," she says. "So we do more diverse kinds of work. We lose members when we stray from the basics."

Organizing can have lots of different faces, argues Ray. "It doesn't matter whether you schedule one-on-one meetings or big parades," he says. "Is it challenging power relations in its own way? If it does that, it's organizing."

Organizing can have lots of different faces, argues Ray. "It doesn't matter whether you schedule one-on-one meetings or big parades," he says. "Is it challenging power relations in its own way? If it does that, it's organizing. Had we been more moderate about the youth center, it might still be here. These people didn't come here to become radical socialists, remember. They came for the American dream."

Megan believes CDC can help people change their lives little by little. There are over fifty-thousand people living in New Mexican colonias, but the dogged nineteen—in the squat white building that houses CDC—have decided, at least for now, that the best way to make improvements is slowly, steadfastly, a few people at a time.

Farm Grows Native Leader

hawaii : manny miles

Amidst the majestic mountains lined with picturesque kukui nut trees and lush flora, Lualualei valley provides a unique setting for an organic farm, Mala 'Ai 'Opio. The farm, more commonly known as MA'O Organic Farms, not only provides food to the local community, but also affords opportunities for young people.

Manny Miles is one such example. He gained work and leadership skills as part of MA'O's Youth Leadership Training Program. A typical teenager, he graduated from high school and planned to attend Bethel College to play soccer. But mixed feelings on what to do with the rest of his life, and the thought of traveling so far from home, put his college plans on hold.

Farming was not on Manny's "top ten" list of career choices, but when the opportunity for an internship arose, he decided to give it a try. Manny went through the program and has worked his way up from student intern to apprentice to farm manager. He began on the farm when he was eighteen and is now twenty-four years old.

"I never thought I'd be a farmer, but always liked working outdoors," he says. His first experiences on the farm left much to be desired, and he admits he "didn't have the love for it yet." A typical sixty-five to seventy hour work week left him drained and exhausted.

Manny now takes college classes and works what he considers part-time, forty hour per week. The garden crops he manages range from bananas, taro, lemons, and mangoes to choi sum, mesclun greens, radishes, and spinach. The goal for MA'O is to have a wide variety of items available for sale at the local farmers' markets.

Although he is pursuing a degree in business, Manny has no intention of abandoning his crops. He prefers being in the field to sitting behind a desk, and hopes to strike a balance where he can spend 70 percent of his time outdoors and 30 percent in an office.

"Working everyday on the farm is easier than going to school. At school, I'm both mentally drained and physically drained," he says.

The serene surroundings of MA'O Organic Farms mask the overdevelopment of the area. Just down the street, in what was recently a rural area, are a McDonald's, Kentucky Fried Chicken, and 7-Eleven. The farm just purchased eleven acres to add to their original five acre plot, and Manny hopes that by obtaining his degree, he will be able to play a larger role in planning for the farm's expansion. Farming the land has changed his life and his thinking. "By working on the farm and growing crops," he says, "I think I can help slow development in the area. The more land I farm, the fewer houses will be built, the less infrastructure. We already have a four-lane highway and six fast food restaurants down the street," he says. "We don't need more." Manny is making better food choices for himself, too, choosing fresh food over fast food and being conscious of where his food comes from.

Among his lessons growing up, Manny's parents taught him about the value of hard work and encouraged his appreciation for community. "My Dad would grow corn for us and for the neighbors," he says. "We learned to take care of the land." Manny's mother is also one of his strongest supporters. He reflects, "She loves gardening and being outdoors, and she encouraged me to stick with it."

As a Native Hawaiian, Manny has also gained a deeper appreciation for his own culture and the 'aina,' or land. "I'm more in tune with the culture," he says. "I take care of the land because later it will take care of me."

The Waianae Community Re-Development Corporation founded MA'O in 2001 as a community food service initiative. MA'O Farm's mission is to develop a comprehensive local food system, to fight hunger, improve nutrition, strengthen local food security, and empower low-income families to move toward self-sufficiency. By implementing the student agricultural program, they hope to enhance the lives of local youth.

The student agricultural program is geared towards individuals between seventeen and twenty-five years of age. It offers training in both leadership and organic farming. Youth are paid part-time wages for working on the farm—a rare opportunity for young people in the Waianae community, where unemployment often runs three times the state average. They are also paid to complete an academic program and receive certification at the local community college. Recruitment begins at the local high schools with kids who really are excited about farming.

"About 90 percent of the kids in this community are remedial in math and English," Manny says. "The farm-to-college program helps them advance their skills." And a lot of the kids that come into the program need motivation and inspiration in order to avoid adverse lifestyles, he adds.

At first, Manny felt like the only kid his age engaged in this type of work, but after attending national and international farming conferences, he has a different perspective: "I don't feel alone in this business anymore. I now have a sense of place and know where I need to go."

"By working on the farm and growing crops, I think I can help slow development in the area.... We already have a four-lane highway and six fast food restaurants down the street; we don't need more."

Shaping Tomorrow's Leaders

delaware : joy mcgrath

During the 1950s and 1960s, pedestrian traffic around the Wilmington, Delaware, farmers' market was so robust that police were called in for crowd control. With Delaware's thriving agricultural community, the farmers' market in Wilmington brought tens of thousands of people to the city to buy fresh products.

"They'd actually have to blow whistles and stop the people so the cars could get through," says Joy McGrath, thirty-two.

Joy grew up just fifteen minutes from Middleton, Delaware, where her grandfather had a fruit and vegetable farm that joined Wilmington's market twice a week. Her father operated the farm as a greenhouse and nursery business.

Today the landscape looks starkly different than it did when Joy was growing up. St. Andrew's boarding high school in Middletown, where Joy is in charge of public relations and fundraising, is being strangled from all sides by suburbanization. Middletown has annexed more than 4000 acres since 1998, and the population has grown from 3800 in 1990 to 11,500 in 2007. In the midst of this development, Joy leads efforts to preserve the school's 1500 acres of prime farmland and more than 600 acres of forest and wetlands.

The McGrath family lost their farm to new highway construction, and Joy's father is now director of farmland preservation for the state of Delaware. With his help, Joy transformed two acres on St. Andrew's campus into a thriving organic garden. Each

afternoon, fifteen to twenty students work outside with Joy—planting, irrigating, and weeding. They produce compost from campus leaf waste, horse manure, and all the nonanimal leftovers. Students harvest salad greens, beets, herbs, squash, tomatoes, peppers, and sweet potatoes for meals in the dining hall, and ultimately return their food scraps to the soil.

"The kids who work in the garden make an announcement at meal times about what food on the menu came from the garden," Joy says. "They always get a huge round of applause from the other kids!"

Before Joy instituted composting in the dining hall, each 360-person meal produced fourteen to fifteen gallons of food waste. "Now we're down to about two gallons, just because of the composting," she says.

"What's critical is that these students in the future, whether they're politicians or lawyers or bankers or doctors, (because they're probably not all going to be farmers), understand that their food is grown somewhere."

The garden is seeping into the school curriculum in amazing and unexpected ways. English classes have come out to help because "if you want to understand a poem Seamus Heaney wrote about digging potatoes, it's hard to do unless you've actually dug potatoes," Joy says. The Chinese class worked on the garden while doing Buddhist work meditations and the girls JV soccer team shovels compost as an alternative to practice.

"We're looking at the campus as a whole system," explains Joy. "That is the bedrock of organic and sustainable production. We're looking for new methods of tillage, new kinds of fertilizer, and new buffers for our ponds. We're taking the two acre organic garden as a model and trying to figure out how to continue that practice."

Joy also sits on St. Andrew's sustainability committee, working to support local food systems. So far the school has succeeded in getting all of its pork products, honey, and a lot of fruits and vegetables from within a hundred-mile radius. In the future, Joy would like to raise free-range chickens at St. Andrew's that could supply eggs and fertilizer, and be used for pest management.

"What's critical is that these students in the future, whether they're politicians or lawyers or bankers or doctors, (because they're probably not all going to be farmers), understand that their food is grown somewhere," Joy says. "That might seem laughable to a lot of people, especially farmers, but I don't think most kids coming to St. Andrew's, as smart as they are, actually understand the practices and economics driving what food they're eating. To be leaders in the U.S. in twenty years, they'll have to understand that."

Babes in the Backcountry

colorado : leslie ross

At 5:30 a.m. in the morning, in below freezing temperatures, three young women are schlepping incredible bundles of ski equipment into the "Astro Sister," as the Babes in the Backcountry call their fourteen-passenger cargo van.

Founded in 1997 by Leslie Ross, Babes in the Backcountry creates a unique learning environment for women to learn technical backcountry skills. The program aims to provide women with the confidence to explore the backcountry on their own.

Leslie, a three-time National Telemark Free Skiing Champion, created Babes so women could find female mentors, and a safe environment to ask questions or learn new skills. In addition to experienced instructors, she hires recent college graduates as interns to help with everything from managing demo gear to community outreach. While Babes encourages women of all ages and abilities to participate, Leslie hopes that her growing network of women mentors will guide and inspire young women in ways that were not available for her and past generations.

The leaders hop into the Astro Sister, and drive to the ski slope to meet the rest of the staff. They begin arriving at 8 a.m. to sign in and gobble down Clif Bars. Each participant explains their experience level and reason for attending the session. As the group settles in, they find a quiet corner for their morning yoga class, giving participants a chance to breathe and transition from hectic city lives to the natural world that now surrounds them.

The Babes' mission goes beyond wilderness technique to embody a holistic experience. Leslie believes that through teaching young women skills for the backcountry, they develop more self-respect and a greater regard for the environment.

She explains, "When people get a real sense of respect for themselves through outdoor training and leadership skills, that's what helps save the countryside, that's what helps us restore the earth."

At 9:30 a.m., the participants meet the staff, break up into skill levels, and head to the hill. The morning is spent on skiing drills with personal feedback. The group reunites for lunch, and then returns to the slopes for the afternoon. The day ends with an Après-Ski party, which includes a table from High Country Conservation Alliance with information on sustainable practices and ways to get involved in the community.

Colorado's New Belgium Brewing Co., one of the organization's sponsors, brings a lot of life to the Après-Ski with materials about their sustainability practices, and of course, plenty of drinks. The Après gathering gives women time to relax and enjoy each other's company, while reminiscing on the adventures of the day and planning their next outing. In the evening, the instructors return the gear to storage, knowing that thirty new Babes have acquired "the adventure bug."

The idea for Babes came to Leslie after finishing college. She was already an avid skier, but wanted to expand her backcountry skills. She began making backcountry skiing trips to the Colorado's Summit Huts Association's wilderness cabins. Looking back, she recalls that it wasn't until she was spending all of her time at the huts that she noticed she was often the only female amongst the groups there. Leslie realized that there was a serious lack of female mentors, so when she began skiing competitively in the free skiing circuit, she was inspired by meeting other strong and accomplished women skiers. At competitions she met mentors and made friends, who now also instruct her courses. In a society in which media tells young women that they must look a certain way, Babes honors all types.

"We provide an environment where you can celebrate whatever level you are at that day," says Leslie. "Rather than worrying, 'Oh, I should be this or I should be that,' at a Babes workshop women can enjoy the opportunity to be outside regardless of their fitness or ability level. It gives people an opportunity to slow down and breathe and start looking at these incredible women that are there."

Holly Holmes, long-time Babes leader, thinks back in awe at her own transformation. When she began leading trips she, like Leslie, was looking to others for mentorship. Now she is amazed to realize that she has become a mentor to other young women.

The face of Kirsten Nelson, a past Babes intern and participant, lights up as she talks about her first hut experience lugging huge loads up the mountain with women she had just met, and how later she and another woman triggered a fake avalanche to practice their rescue skills. Kirsten worked with Babes for six months after graduating from college. She explains how inspiring it was to her to be surrounded by such humble,

The Babes' mission goes beyond wilderness technique to embody a holistic experience. Leslie believes that through teaching young women skills for the backcountry, they develop more self-respect and a greater regard for the environment.

amazing women. Kirsten finished her internship, but she remains in close contact with the Babes community.

Babes is running a new program this year that targets the growing Latino population in the region. They are collaborating with Latino organizations in the Breckenridge area to enable Latina women to explore the local backcountry. Babes will run clinics with a group of Latinas throughout the winter, beginning with team-building activities and basic wilderness skills, such as learning about appropriate clothing, nutrition, and gear. The group will eventually move outside to practice snowshoeing. The program will end with an overnight snowshoe trip to a hut in the mountains. Leslie trusts that this program will give young Latina women a better sense of where they now live as well as the tools to participate in their new community. This program also helps unite the various communities that live in the mountains of Summit County.

This winter season alone, Babes will host thirty telemark and backcountry skills clinics in Colorado, California, Utah, Canada, Europe, and South America. Some programs are day clinics at local ski mountains; others are overnight trips to the huts or longer backcountry adventures. Leslie is currently working out details for a trip to Japan.

Babes is in the process of becoming a registered nonprofit and runs on the hard work of its leaders, interns, and a host of dedicated volunteers. Leslie is adamant in her praise of her ten major sponsors: Patagonia, Black Diamond, Backcountry Access, Bridgedale, Clif Bar, High Gear, New Belgium, Osprey, Scarpa, and Smith—without whom none of these projects and workshops could have happened.

Kirsten sings the praises of Babes, adding, "I think Babes is a great organization. It has the potential to grow and go many directions allowing women to become involved. When you're with them, you see the world in a better light."

"When people get a real sense of respect for themselves through outdoor training and leadership skills, that's what helps save the countryside, that's what helps us restore the earth."

From Fields to Freedom

florida : gerardo reyes

Gerardo Reyes, thirty-one, Leonel Perez, twenty-one, and the 4000 members of the laborer-run Coalition of Immokalee Workers (CIW) aim to end modern-day slavery in the U.S. and improve exploitative wages and working conditions.

Tomato picking brought Gerardo to the humid, hot fields of Immokalee in south-central Florida when he was twenty-one. Born in Mexico, he came north pursuing the American Dream. Gerardo quickly experienced the harsh realities faced by the laborers who handpick most of America's fruit and vegetables. Workers get up at 4 a.m. and gather in the quiet morning darkness at a square where day-labor contractors come to recruit workers. Ten to fourteen hours later, they return home, bone tired.

A worker needs to pick roughly two tons of tomatoes a day to earn fifty dollars, no easy task—especially in sweltering heat. With such low wages, it's not surprising that living conditions are dismal. Eight to fifteen people often share one cramped trailer. But like many Americans, these people are working to support their families and can't afford to lose their jobs.

When one of Gerardo's day-labor contractors refused to pay him, he moved on to picking oranges. He might have just continued on to the next harvest had he not met a group of determined workers. These individuals, members of the Coalition for Immokalee Workers (CIW), were pursuing a court case against their *patrones* (bosses) for forcing them into modern-day slavery. Gerardo, deeply inspired by their struggle for justice, realized that their struggle was his struggle and decided to join them.

For the millions of women and men who handpick America's food, abuse by contract labor bosses is a fact of life. People desperate for work can be led into debt bondage and outright slavery like an echo of that which existed 150 years ago in these same fields. That contractors would simply refuse to pay workers may seem incredible, but it is not uncommon. One of CIW's first important victories was against such contractors, who were ordered to return over $100,000 in stolen wages.

CIW's members are predominantly *campesinos* (rural farmers) from Mexico, Guatemala, and Haiti. In Immokalee's hot fields and dusty trailer parks, workers converse in native languages like Mixtec, K'iche, Yucatec, Tzotzil, Nahuatl, Zapotec, and Haitian Creole, as well as Spanish. The Immokalee workers, like other migrant laborers, may move from different crops and fields in the course of a week, climbing on board whichever contractor's truck will offer them a paying job. Despite the incredible diversity of backgrounds and languages among CIW's members, they unite and campaign for a common cause.

Leonel Perez of CIW speaks with an authority beyond his twenty-one years: "In the fields, when your boss mistreats and abuses you, you realize you have no voice. In this moment, you can't tell the boss your rights because they'll fire you, or worse. But if all the workers get together, we realize that we have a voice and we aren't afraid to speak."

After numerous strikes, marches, rallies, and fasting, CIW achieved significant victories and began to gain a modicum of respect and dignity in Immokalee. Yet they knew that many others toiled in horrific conditions for far below minimum wage and—worst of all—in silence. As more farmworkers came to CIW seeking help, the organization started formally investigating human rights abuses in the picking fields. Between 1997 and 2008, they helped bring six modern-day slavery operations to justice, freeing over a thousand people from bondage. In some cases, they assisted FBI sting operations aimed against forced labor. In other cases, they helped trapped workers escape from slavery. They can attest that segments of the agricultural system exploit the poverty of day laborers regardless of whether they are U.S. citizens, legal residents, legal refugees, or undocumented workers.

Keeping a labor movement alive, let alone victorious, with such diverse and migratory members is tough, but Gerardo smiles at the challenge. "We take our disadvantages and make them into advantages," he says. Each season, 4000 CIW members disperse across the fruit and vegetable fields of America and bring with them their hands-on experience championing their rights through popular education and organizing. They inform and educate new workers and, sometimes, return with new stories of abuses that merit CIW investigation and legal action.

After victories in Immokalee, CIW determined that the only way to make lasting change in the exploitative agricultural system harming their community was to address the problem on a national scale. Instead of focusing on the local contractors who pay (and sometimes don't pay) America's migrant agricultural laborers, CIW focused on the corporation that buys the most tomatoes: Yum! Brands. Yum! Brands is the world's largest restaurant company—owning chains like KFC, Taco Bell, Pizza Hut, and Long John Silvers. They have over 36,000 restaurants in 110 different countries.

CIW's goal was colossal: to get Yum! Brands to establish higher wage requirements and codes of conduct by the companies from which it buys tomatoes. Against all odds, they initiated their campaign in 2001, focusing on Taco Bell, the corporation's flagship franchise. CIW's strategy was to get the company to pay a penny per

pound more for tomatoes, up from a price that had been stagnant since 1978. The extra penny per pound would go to increase wages for Florida farmworkers.

After four years of refusing to negotiate, Yum! conceded to CIW's demands in 2005 amidst a hail of negative press. This small Floridian band of predominantly young, impoverished, non-English speaking migrant farmworkers had won a victory unique in the history of U.S. labor organizing. Next, they successfully went after McDonalds in 2007, and Burger King, Chipotle, and Whole Foods in 2008, negotiating with each one to raise tomato prices and establish codes of conduct in their supply chains.

CIW maintains their campaigns so stubbornly and successfully because of their remarkable leaderless, consensus-based, decision-making model and their ability to form alliances with groups all across the U.S. and the world. Ever since CIW declared the nationwide boycott of Taco Bell, help began arriving from concerned student groups, activist organizations, musicians, church groups, the Congressional Hispanic Caucus, and even President Jimmy Carter. CIW also took their message on the road, sending once-shy campesino youth leaders like Gerardo out to speak to thousands at conferences and rallies.

The CIW's central committee now consists of thirty-five male and female farmworkers. Their campaigns have inspired other human rights and food advocacy organizations across the country to join them. These are not privileged activists paid by respected NGOs: these are average American farmworkers who put in long days in the field and then volunteer to meet at night to organize for the rights of their compañeros from all races and backgrounds across America.

"But if all the workers get together, we realize that we have a voice and we aren't afraid to speak."

Gerardo takes their success in stride, indeed the struggles of migrant farmworkers have a long way to go. His parents and grand parents were campesinos in Mexico, small farmers who lived off the land and loved working the earth. Far from being ashamed to call himself a seasonal farmworker, Gerardo and all the CIW compañeros take conspicuous pride in their work and occupation. "Working the earth is good; the plants, the vegetables are good—but the industry treats us badly. Many workers are consumed in misery and poverty, humiliated by contractors and companies, and we want to change this. The hard work we do shouldn't make anyone ashamed, it should make them proud."

The Barking Moon Researcher

oregon : melissa matthewson

In 1987, when Melissa Matthewson reached the age of ten, the California, citrus-grove-filled landscape that epitomized her childhood was gone. She had become a child of suburbia.

The days Melissa longed for were the ones her father strived to forget. Her dad was raised on a struggling farm, where hard work wasn't a choice, but a meager means of subsistence. He grew up with bitter memories of farm life, while Melissa has been left with an equally sour taste of suburbia.

The realm of taste, though, is the one area where farming does make sense to her dad. A lifetime "foodie," he would sometimes take Melissa to the farmers' market in Santa Monica to buy select produce. Today, a freshly picked tomato from her garden at Barking Moon Farm in Applegate, Oregon, tastefully creates an understanding between father and daughter.

Barking Moon Farm is in the valley of Thompson Creek, which feeds the Applegate River in Southern Oregon's greater Rogue Valley. Josh, Melissa's husband, runs the ten-acre farm full time. A new mom, Melissa works part time on the farm and part time at Oregon State University's Southern Oregon Research & Extension Center (SOREC), where she codirects the Small Farms Program.

The first white farmers of the Applegate Valley area were primarily ranchers who managed large tracts of rangeland for their cattle, while growing hay for feed. As the greater Rogue Valley transformed from range to cropland, largely producing pears and apples, Oregon State University Extension established the SOREC experiment station in the early 1900s. In 2005, OSU Extension recognized a new trend: the total acreage being farmed in Oregon was going down, yet the number of small family farmers was on the rise. In response, they created several Small Farms Extension positions, including the one Melissa now holds.

Barking Moon is one of the twelve member farms that form the Siskiyou Sustainable Cooperative CSA (Community Supported Agriculture). Together, they provide weekly boxes of produce to customers who pay a set fee for their share of the yearly harvest. This win-win arrangement gives customers fresh, local, organic produce at a reasonable price while the farmers receive a guaranteed income.

Melissa and Josh farm two and a half acres of organic vegetables, and plan to expand another acre into perennial crops like fruit trees and cane fruit. On another two acres, they keep 100 organically fed, pasture-raised hens. Besides the Siskiyou CSA, they sell at two local farmers' markets, run their own small CSA, and provide produce to several restaurants in the Rogue Valley. They also sponsor two "Within Earthly Bounds" (WEB) organic farming interns.

Like Melissa, most young people grow up disconnected from the rural countryside. If they dream of a different life, it is hard to know where to start. When

Melissa was eighteen, she attended the University of California at Santa Cruz where she studied agroecology. She went on to get a master's degree in environmental studies from the University of Montana. While in graduate school, Melissa worked on an assessment of the Missoula food system and on the student organic farm. She and Josh also worked as interns on Whistling Duck Farm in 2005. This local farm is where they really learned the ins and outs of organic agriculture and how to be successful, small-scale farmers.

In 2006, Melissa began working with OSU Extension, the same year she and Josh purchased Barking Moon Farm. Melissa credits her career path to an afternoon at the University of Santa Cruz Kresge Food Cooperative. As a freshman in college, she volunteered for a membership drive and was astonished by the beauty and quality of fresh, local produce grown by organic farmers. This is when she realized her love for food and farming.

Now on her farm and through her OSU Extension position, Melissa feeds people—with food and knowledge. She works with all types of farmers, but specializes in new and beginning farms. She helps them to develop niche enterprises, like small-scale pastured poultry or market gardens. She helps them plan their businesses and develop their customer base. She also helps them to better care for the land with classes on weed and pasture management, soil quality, and livestock management.

Melissa has learned how to be a better listener and facilitator, not pushing personal farming beliefs, but allowing herself to be a neutral resource. She helps farmers choose the best path for their individual situation. What sustains her personally is knowing she is makes a difference, whether it's helping to keep a small farmer in business, creating a local food network, or turning someone on to a new idea.

"New ideas are born out of people getting together," Melissa says, "and that's a key part of rural living. Your neighbors are important to you, whether it's an emergency or a harvest celebration. Your livelihoods are intimately connected to the land and to being a resource for one another."

"New ideas are born out of people getting together, and that's a key part of rural living. Your neighbors are important to you, whether it's an emergency or a harvest celebration."

writers and photographers credits

cover

Cover Photography: *Ragan Sutterfield*, Dave Holman; *Black Pot Cookoff and Festival musician*, Dave Holman; *Roy and Kaylee Benjamin*, Kiki Hubbard; *Natalie Smith*, Chad A. Stevens. Spine: *Backcountry Babes* Back Cover, Jessica Marsan. *Extravaganza Crew*, Dave Holman; *Backcountry Babes*, Jessica Marsan; *Noemi Alverez*, Nathalie Jordi; *South Dakota Lakota builders*, Dave Holman

front pages

Photography: p.2; Dave Holman - *Amadou Diop, Beatrice and Tracy Hayhurst, Jesse and Betsy Meerman*; Brett Olson - *Olivia*. *p.6*, Dave Holman - *Nick Tilsen*; Loretta Reed - *Kathi Wines*; Brett Olson - *Axel*

introduction

Photography: *p. 8*; Dave Holman - *Raina Webber*. p.9, Dave Holman - *John Jordan, Nick Tilsen, Beatrice Hayhurst*; Brad Christensen - *Lisa Dardy McGee*

one : farming for the future

Photography: p.10; Courtesy of Full Belly Farm - *Farmers from Full Belly Farm*; Hailey Branson - *Travis Schnaithman*; Dave Holman - *Lohrs Orchard, Beatrice and Tracy Hayhurst*

Before Organic : South Carolina
Writer: Nathalie Jordi
Photography: Dave Holman, p.12 - *Shaheed Harris*, p.13 - *Sorting seeds*, p.14 - *Shaheed Harris in the garden*

A Piece of Rural Perfection : California
Writer: Mele Anderson
Photography: Courtesy of Full Belly Farm, p.16 - *Joaquina Jacobo*

An Independent Path : Minnesota
Writer: Laura Borgendale
Photography: Laura Borgendale, p.18 - *Jason, Ian, Aiden and Laura Penner*, p.19 - *Sows and piglets*; p.20 - *Jason and piglets*

Survival Take Roots : New Hampshire
Writer: Heather Foran
Photography: Dave Holman, p.21 - *Calf feeding*, p.22-23 - *Frozen dairy*

The Noisy Little Farmer : Connecticut
Writer: Dave Holman
Photography: Dave Holman, p.24 - *Beatrice, Dan, and Tracy Hayhurst*, p.25 - *Chubby Bunny Farm*, p.26 - *Dan Hayhurst*, p.27 - *Pig in throne*

Hay Bales & Five Generations : Oklahoma
Writer: Hailey Branson
Photography: Hailey Branson, p.27 - *Travis and Tyler Schnaithman*, p.28-29 - *Loading haywagon*

Herbs and Heritage : Texas
Writer: Nathalie Jordi
Photography: Nathalie Jordi, p.31 - *Noemi Alverez*, p.32 *Noemi with her parents, Sylvia and Miguel*, p.32-33 *Gardens*

Vast Promise in Montana : Montana
Writer: Kiki Hubbard
Photography: Kiki Hubbard, p.34 - *Roy and Kaylee Benjamin*, p.35 - *Roy with his truck*, p.35-36 - *Montana landscape*

Farm Fun & Education Fight Sprawl : Maryland
Writer: Dave Holman
Photography: Dave Holman, p.37 - *Candace Lohr*, p.38 - *Picking apples*

two : flourishing entrepreneurs

Photography: p.40, Dave Holman - *Ben Graham*

Wheels of Change in a Rural Town : Indiana
Writer: Dave Holman
Photography: Dave Holman, p.42, 43 - *Cain Bond*

A Tasty Enterprise : Utah
Writer: Nathalie Jordi
Photography: Elaine Borgen, p.44 - *Andrew Dayish*, p.45 - *Chocolates*, p.46 - *Hubert, VP of sales and marketing*

From Mines to Wines : Virginia
Writer: Alessandra Vitrella
Photography: Dave Holman, p.47 - *Dave Lawson*, p.48-49 - *Vineyard*

New Ideas, Old-Time Values : Kansas
Writer: Margaret Pendleton
Photography: Maralee Bauman, p.50 - *Rosanna Bauman*, p.51 - *Marvin (top), Joanna with a goat (bottom)*, p.52 - *Kevin (top), Steven (bottom)*, p.53 - *Ivin*

From Greenhouse to Grocery : Missouri
Writer: Bryce Oates
Photography: Brett Olson, p.56 - *Veggies*

Simple Materials, Grand Designs : Vermont
Writer: Dave Holman
Photography: Dave Holman, p.57- *Ben Graham*, p.58-59 - *Bonfire*, p.60 - *Ben Graham*

A Farm Fresh Innovator : Rhode Island
Writer: Dave Holman
Photography: Dave Holman, p.61 - *Louella Hill*, p.62-63 - *Farmers' market (top), Harvesting in the rain (bottom)*

three : embracing heritage

Photography: p.64; Dave Holman- *South Dakota activist*; Loretta Reed - *Kathi Wines*; Dave Holman - *Dakwa Woodruff*

Reviving Tradition : Washington
Writer: Dave Holman
Photography: Dave Holman, p.66 - *Dakwa Woodruff*, p.69 - *Shilaily*; Brett Olson, *Orca pod*

Passionately Preserving Place : West Virginia
Writer: Alessandra Vitrella
Photography: Dave Holman, p.70-71 - *Hanna Thurman*

From Sun Dance to Community Plans : South Dakota
Writer: Dave Holman
Photography: Dave Holman, p.73 - *Nick Tilsen*, p.74-75 - *Building for the future*

A Sustainable Catch : Maine
Writer: Dave Holman
Photography: Dave Holman, p.76 - *John Jordan*, p.77 - *John Jordan and Mark McGoon*, p.78 - *Emptying lobster pots*

Ranching Poetic : Nevada
Writer: Heather Kennison
Photography: Loretta Reed, p.79, 81 - *Kathi Wines*

index